Sencha Touch 2 Up and Running

Adrian Kosmaczewski

O'REILLY®

Beijing · Cambridge · Farnham · Köln · Sebastopol · Tokyo

Sencha Touch 2 Up and Running

by Adrian Kosmaczewski

Published by O'Reilly Media, Inc., 1005 Gravenstein Highway North, Sebastopol, CA 95472.

O'Reilly books may be purchased for educational, business, or sales promotional use. Online editions are also available for most titles (*http://my.safaribooksonline.com*). For more information, contact our corporate/institutional sales department: 800-998-9938 or *corporate@oreilly.com*.

Editors: Simon St. Laurent and Meghan Blanchette
Production Editor: Melanie Yarbrough

Proofreader: Julie Van Keuren
Indexer: Judy McConville
Cover Designer: Karen Montgomery
Interior Designer: David Futato
Illustrator: Rebecca Demarest

March 2013:   First Edition

Revision History for the First Edition:

2013-02-12   First release

See *http://oreilly.com/catalog/errata.csp?isbn=9781449339388* for release details.

ISBN: 978-1-449-33938-8

[LSI]

This book is dedicated with love and gratitude to Claudia. Te amo, preciosa.

Table of Contents

Preface

The world of JavaScript frameworks is a ground in constant motion. New libraries and packages are published nearly every day, but as in any other market, only a few of them strive to attain a relatively large audience, reaching millions of downloads and, in some cases, some sort of cult following.

Sencha Touch is, without any doubt, one of the most talked-about of those frameworks —sometimes loved, sometimes hated, but never ignored. Released to the public in 2010 after two years in the making, it is in many respects the most advanced touchscreen-enabled JavaScript framework available today. It is also a daunting platform, with an incredible amount of functionality baked in, covering almost every possible requirement in the process of developing mobile applications.

This book hopes to provide a meaningful, simple path to approach the complexity encapsulated in this system, allowing developers to create mobile applications for iOS, Android, and BlackBerry devices.

Intended Audience

This book is a general introduction to the Sencha Touch framework and platform, intended for mobile developers familiar with either iOS or Android who have an intermediate or advanced level of knowledge of JavaScript.

Structure of this Book

The book is structured as follows:

- Chapter 1, "Getting Started," provides a complete overview of the framework. Developers who are in a hurry or who want to get down to the code can read this chapter to get a feeling of what the platform is capable of.

- Chapter 2, "The Class System," starts with a discussion of the particular flavor of the model-view-controller (MVC) architecture used and enforced by Sencha Touch applications. It provides an introduction to the class definition and instantiation paradigm, and finally it contains an extensive review of low-level foundation code provided by the framework (data structures, algorithms, application programming interfaces [APIs], etc.)

- Chapter 3, "Views," contains a description of the extensive library of visual components provided by Sencha Touch, including examples and sample code. It also discusses the approach required to create your own components from scratch.

- Chapter 4, "Data," explains in detail how to define and use model classes in your applications, including a discussion of the whole infrastructure of stores, proxies, validations, and associations.

- Chapter 5, "Forms," builds upon the previous two chapters to discuss in detail the creation and use of complex forms in applications, including a complete description of every type of form field available.

- Chapter 6, "Controllers," provides the final elements of the Sencha Touch MVC architecture, explaining how to encapsulate business logic using controller objects, highlighting the benefits of this approach.

- Chapter 7, "Styling Applications," explains how to use Sass to embellish and give a unique visual personality to applications, including a reference to the most important variables and elements that can be modified by application designers.

- Chapter 8, "Debugging, Testing, and Documenting," shows how to increase the quality of Sencha Touch applications using tools such as the WebKit Web Inspector, Jasmine, Siesta, and JSDuck.

- Chapter 9, "Sencha Architect," provides an introduction to this commercial tool that provides both an integrated development environment (IDE) and a visual application designer canvas, used for rapid application development.

- Finally, Chapter 10, "Deployment in Devices," explains how to distribute Sencha Touch applications in production, either as HTML5 offline apps or as standalone native apps for iOS and Android, to be sold through the respective marketplaces of those platforms.

Code of the Book

You can download all the code samples of this book from Github (*https://github.com/akosma/Sencha-Touch-2-Up-And-Running*). The project contains an installation script named install.sh that will download all the required libraries for the samples to run. The code of the book is distributed using a liberal Berkeley Source Distribution (BSD) license, and will be updated to reflect any changes and updates to Sencha Touch 2.x.

> Please be aware that the code samples are meant to be run from a web server, and not just by double-clicking and opening the index.html file in your browser directly. This is because Sencha Touch uses the XMLHTTPRequest object, which cannot be used when opening files using the file:/// protocol.

Conventions Used in This Book

The following typographical conventions are used in this book:

Italic
 Indicates new terms, URLs, email addresses, filenames, and file extensions.

Constant width
 Used for program listings, as well as within paragraphs to refer to program elements such as variable or function names, databases, data types, environment variables, statements, and keywords.

Constant width bold
 Shows commands or other text that should be typed literally by the user.

Constant width italic
 Shows text that should be replaced with user-supplied values or by values determined by context.

> This icon signifies a tip, suggestion, or general note.

> This icon indicates a warning or caution.

Using Code Examples

This book is here to help you get your job done. In general, if this book includes code examples, you may use the code in this book in your programs and documentation. You do not need to contact us for permission unless you're reproducing a significant portion of the code. For example, writing a program that uses several chunks of code from this book does not require permission. Selling or distributing a CD-ROM of examples from O'Reilly books does require permission. Answering a question by citing this book and quoting example code does not require permission. Incorporating a significant amount of example code from this book into your product's documentation does require permission.

We appreciate, but do not require, attribution. An attribution usually includes the title, author, publisher, and ISBN. For example: "*Sencha Touch 2 Up and Running* by Adrian Kosmaczewski (O'Reilly). Copyright 2013 Adrian Kosmaczewski, 978-1-449-33938-8."

If you feel your use of code examples falls outside fair use or the permission given above, feel free to contact us at *permissions@oreilly.com*.

Safari® Books Online

 Safari Books Online is an on-demand digital library that delivers expert content in both book and video form from the world's leading authors in technology and business.

Technology professionals, software developers, web designers, and business and creative professionals use Safari Books Online as their primary resource for research, problem solving, learning, and certification training.

Safari Books Online offers a range of product mixes and pricing programs for organizations, government agencies, and individuals. Subscribers have access to thousands of books, training videos, and prepublication manuscripts in one fully searchable database from publishers like O'Reilly Media, Prentice Hall Professional, Addison-Wesley Professional, Microsoft Press, Sams, Que, Peachpit Press, Focal Press, Cisco Press, John Wiley & Sons, Syngress, Morgan Kaufmann, IBM Redbooks, Packt, Adobe Press, FT Press, Apress, Manning, New Riders, McGraw-Hill, Jones & Bartlett, Course Technology, and dozens more. For more information about Safari Books Online, please visit us online.

How to Contact Us

Please address comments and questions concerning this book to the publisher:

O'Reilly Media, Inc.
1005 Gravenstein Highway North
Sebastopol, CA 95472
800-998-9938 (in the United States or Canada)
707-829-0515 (international or local)
707-829-0104 (fax)

We have a web page for this book, where we list errata, examples, and any additional information. You can access this page at *http://oreil.ly/sencha_touch_2*.

To comment or ask technical questions about this book, send email to *bookques tions@oreilly.com*.

For more information about our books, courses, conferences, and news, see our website at *http://www.oreilly.com*.

Find us on Facebook: *http://facebook.com/oreilly*

Follow us on Twitter: *http://twitter.com/oreillymedia*

Watch us on YouTube: *http://www.youtube.com/oreillymedia*

Acknowledgments

The idea for this book came as soon as my previous one, *Mobile JavaScript Application Development* went to press. In that book I had included a short introduction to Sencha Touch, and writing that chapter was such an enjoyable experience that I thought a full book on the subject was a worthy goal.

Frederick Brooks famously explained the consequences of the "second-system effect," where small, successful systems have absolutely monstrous successors; I can say that this book suffered from a similar pathology, maybe because I wrote it amid one of the most complex and difficult times of my life.

Because of this context, this second book would never have been possible without the great help of lots of incredible people scattered all over the planet: to begin with, the whole Sencha team, who have created and documented an out-of-this-planet kind of JavaScript framework; kudos and thanks to all of them, in particular to Jeff Hartley, vice president of services; to David Marsland, chief instructor; and Jim Soper, senior technical trainer at Sencha.

I would also like to thank Simon St. Laurent, my editor at O'Reilly, who wholeheartedly embraced the idea of this book just as we were sending *Mobile JavaScript Application Development* to press, and was extremely supportive during the process. I would also like to thank the reviewers of this book: Jens-Christian Fischer, from Zurich, Switzerland, with whom I had the privilege of teaching Sencha Touch in the past, and who has provided me with incredible tips and tricks to make this book a better one; Mats Bryntse, founder of Bryntum AB from Lund, Sweden, creator of the Siesta testing framework described in Chapter 8, and who reviewed that chapter extensively; Gabriel García Marengo, web designer at IMD in Lausanne, Switzerland, who sent great feedback, and who is one of the best friends anyone could have; Martín Paoletta, solutions architect at Redbee in Buenos Aires, Argentina, who read the book from the perspective of a solution provider and made excellent recommendations. Thanks to you all.

## CHAPTER 1

Getting Started

This chapter will give you an introduction to Sencha Touch, the framework, the platform, and its developer experience. It will take you through the required steps to install the tools in your workstation and will guide you through the creation of your first basic applications.

What Is Sencha Touch?

Sencha Touch (*http://www.sencha.com/products/touch*) is an MVC JavaScript framework specially designed to create mobile web applications for touchscreen devices. Sencha Touch allows developers to create applications for mobile platforms that feature web browsers implementing the latest standards, like the WebKit (*http://www.webkit.org/*) browser engine.

 At the time of this writing, the latest available version of Sencha Touch was version 2.1.

Sencha Touch is a rather large framework, which may look daunting to JavaScript developers used to smaller, leaner libraries such as jQuery or Prototype. Sencha Touch is conceived as a whole package, including most services and functions offered by other frameworks, and it can be easily extended in many different ways to accommodate the needs of developers in different areas of expertise. You typically do not need to use other libraries than Sencha Touch in your project; if you need a certain utility, you can be sure that the framework includes it by default.

The explicit choice of WebKit is an interesting one; the Sencha Touch team has taken a deliberate decision not to support other mobile browser engines, such as Gecko (Firefox), Presto (Opera), or Trident (Internet Explorer). The exclusive support of modern browsers allows Sencha Touch to use many of the most advanced web technologies available today.

This choice also affects the developer experience, because only Safari or Google Chrome can be used to debug Sencha Touch applications on a desktop environment like Linux, Windows, or OS X.

Internet Explorer 10 support
The Sencha team has recently announced (*http://www.sencha.com/blog/sencha-touch-with-windows-phone-8*) the support for Internet Explorer 10 for Windows Phone 8 in Sencha Touch 2.2, not yet available at the time of this writing.

What Kind of Applications Can You Build with It?

Apple, in one of the first versions of its iOS design guidelines document (*http://developer.apple.com/library/ios/#documentation/userexperience/conceptual/mobilehig/Introduction/Introduction.html*), famously stated that there are three major kinds of mobile applications that could be created for the iPhone:

- Utility apps, like weather or stocks information apps
- Productivity apps, like business or document-oriented applications
- Immersive apps, like games

Following this simple taxonomy, Sencha Touch is most suited for delivering applications of the first two kinds. Although it is certainly possible to create games or other types of apps featuring complex user experiences, this book covers only the creation of utility and productivity applications.

Finally, Sencha Touch allows developers to create applications for mobile touchscreen devices—that is, smartphones and tablets—but it can be used to create desktop applications as well.

A Bit of History

Back in 2005, the Web 2.0 movement was starting to radically transform the notion of web content. Ajax-enabled sites like Gmail showed the public that a new type of interaction was possible, that a new kind of content could be shown in regular web pages without using proprietary plug-ins. Douglas Crockford was explaining that JavaScript was a great language misunderstood by many (*http://www.crockford.com/javascript/javascript.html*), and libraries like script.aculo.us and Prototype (*http://prototypejs.org*) were offering developers concrete and solid grounds for cross-browser masterpieces.

Amidst all the fuss, Yahoo! released the first version of its YUI library (*http://yuilibrary.com*), allowing developers to create complex, "desktop-like" applications across operating systems and browsers. YUI can be considered a seminal work, after which several other libraries appeared through the years.

Around that time, Jack Slocum started working on a set of extensions for YUI called YUI-Ext. After a couple of releases, the interest in his library grew so much that he removed the requirement of YUI altogether, making the library able to use Prototype or YUI for lower-level cross-browser compatibility.

Ext JS (*http://www.sencha.com/products/extjs*) was born. For years, Ext JS set the standard in terms of cross-browser compatibility and design, allowing developers to create complex browser applications in a fraction of the time, and without having to care about browser incompatibility problems. In 2009, the company behind Ext JS incorporated as Sencha Inc., with headquarters in Redwood City, California.

In 2009, the rise of the touchscreen smartphone and, later, the iPad, prompted the Ext JS team to create a version of the framework geared exclusively for these new devices; the result of their efforts is Sencha Touch, released in version 1.0 at the end of 2010.

The first version of Sencha Touch was not completely compatible with the contemporary version of Ext JS, and it was also criticized for its relatively low performance benchmarks, particularly in old devices such as the iPhone 3G. To address these issues, Sencha Touch 2 was released in March 2012, providing a brand-new rendering engine based 100% on Cascading Style Sheets (CSS), and a new class system compatible with Ext JS 4.

Main Features

Sencha Touch is more than just a full-featured framework geared toward the creation of utilities and productivity applications; it is actually a complete enterprise web application platform, with the following characteristics:

- Large UI library widget, largely inspired by iOS, both in design and functionality
- Fast rendering engine based on CSS, which can be hardware-accelerated in the latest mobile devices
- Well-defined architecture, enforcing the MVC architecture from the very beginning
- Built-in connectors for network data services, such as Representational State Tranfer (REST) web services, and support for offline mobile web applications
- Advanced class-loading mechanism, enforcing naming guidelines and the MVC architecture
- A command-line build system, managing merging and minification of application code, as well as building native applications for Android and iOS

- Extensive documentation, available as a set of dynamic HTML pages, including searching and filtering features without requiring any server-side infrastructure

Sencha Touch can be seen as an "all-in-one" framework, including all the APIs and tools required to create your mobile applications.

Device and Browser Support

Sencha Touch, at the moment of this writing, supports only the following mobile platforms:

- iOS since version 3
- Android since version 2.3
- BlackBerry OS since version 6 (only for devices featuring WebKit-powered browsers)

Furthermore, the Sencha Touch team has announced the upcoming availability of support for Windows Phone 8 (*http://www.sencha.com/blog/sencha-touch-with-windows-phone-8*) in 2013, as well as a preliminary version of a theme for BlackBerry 10 (*http://www.sencha.com/blog/introducing-sencha-touch-2-1-and-more/*).

Sencha Touch is a 100% browser-based framework, and as such it is server-agnostic; you can deploy your Sencha Touch applications using any server-side technology, like PHP, Java, Ruby on Rails, .NET, or any other stack of your choice.

Sencha Touch 2.1 Exclusively
This book will deal exclusively with the APIs and features of Sencha Touch 2.1, without making any references to the characteristics of previous versions of this framework.

Licensing

Sencha Touch is available under a quite complex licensing scheme (*http://www.sencha.com/products/touch/license/*); at the time of this writing, developers can use the framework as follows.

On open source projects:

- If you plan to distribute your application fully disclosing the source code, there is a version of Sencha Touch distributed through the GPLv3 license.
- If you do not wish to use the GPLv3 license, there is a Free Libre and Open Source (FLOSS) license available as well.

On commercial projects:

- You can use Sencha Touch for free, without any fees, either per application, per user or per developer.
- For embedded applications, you can use Sencha Touch for free up to 5,000 installations.
- Finally, a commercial OEM license is available as well, for companies willing to distribute Sencha Touch as part of their own commercial applications or services.

Sencha Touch is also distributed and licensed as part of the "Sencha Complete" (*http://www.sencha.com/products/complete/*) package, which includes the following:

- Sencha Touch and Ext JS developer licenses
- Sencha Charts, briefly described in Chapter 3
- Sencha Eclipse plug-in
- Sencha Cmd
- Support tickets
- A license of use of Sencha Architect, an application visual design tool, described in detail in Chapter 9

Installing the Developer Environment

To create applications with Sencha Touch, you need the following tools, many of those part of the standard web developer toolkit:

- A computer running Linux, OS X, or Windows
- Google Chrome or Apple Safari
- A text editor
- The Sencha Touch framework
- A working Ruby and RubyGems installation

And that is pretty much everything you need to start with. Of course, Sencha Touch being a mobile framework, you might want to have either the Android or the iOS software development kit (SDK), both available for free from Google and Apple respectively. And, last but not least, a mobile device, running iOS or Android, in order to test your applications on the device. For the moment you do not need the mobile device or the SDK; although handy, you can just use your desktop browser (based on WebKit) to run the application as is.

Other tools are recommended to accelerate your developer workflow. In particular, the example code of this book was written on a Mac running OS X Mountain Lion, plus some other tools:

- iOS Simulator bundled with Xcode 4.5 (available for free in the Mac App Store)
- Homebrew (*http://mxcl.github.com/homebrew/*)
- Google Chrome (*http://www.google.com/chrome*)
- iTerm2 (*http://www.iterm2.com/*), Zsh (*http://www.zsh.org/*), oh-my-zsh (*https:// github.com/robbyrussell/oh-my-zsh*), and tmux (*http://tmux.sourceforge.net/*)
- Vim (*http://www.vim.org*) and MacVim (*http://code.google.com/p/macvim/*) with the Janus plug-in distribution (*https://github.com/carlhuda/janus*)
- LiveReload (*http://livereload.com/*)
- MAMP Pro (*http://www.mamp.info/en/mamp-pro/*)
- iOS devices (iPhone and iPad)

The combination of MacVim (plus the JavaScriptLint plug-in) and LiveReload are huge boosters to productivity, but of course your mileage may vary.

Of course, the next thing you need is the actual Sencha Touch library. If you go to the Sencha website, you can get a ZIP file directly from the home page; however, pay attention to the fact that you are going to be asked about the license for your project. In this case, we are going to browse the official download page of Sencha Touch (*http:// www.sencha.com/products/touch/download/*) to get the GPLv3 version, the one we are going to use throughout this book to show examples.

Installation script

The source code of the application, available in Github (*https:// github.com/akosma/Sencha-Touch-2-Up-And-Running*), contains a script (install.sh) for Unix systems, which automatically downloads and installs the required libraries for the samples to work.

Sencha Touch Distribution

Once downloaded, open the ZIP file; inside you will have several different folders. The most important are the following ones:

- Several JavaScript files are available in the root of the distribution folder: Among them, sencha-touch-all-debug.js and sencha-touch-all.js are the most important, used during both development and production. The biggest difference between them is that the -debug version is not minified, which makes it easier to pinpoint and troubleshoot errors in your applications as you develop them.

- The docs folder contains a complete documentation system, ready to use, available offline for your perusal; later in this chapter we are going to describe in detail the different features of this documentation system.

- The examples folder contains lots of sample applications built with Sencha Touch, each showcasing a particular aspect of the framework. It is strongly recommended to try them all, particularly the Kitchen Sink application (located in examples/kitchensink), which is a complete demo of all the widgets available in the Sencha Touch framework.

- The resources folder contains not only pre-built CSS files and images provided by the framework, but also the complete list of SASS source files used to generate those CSS styles. In a later chapter we are going to study in detail how to customize your Sencha Touch application, creating your own styles for your applications.

- Finally, the src folder contains the original JavaScript source files of the Sencha Touch framework, used to generate the final, minified JavaScript files that you will actually use to power your own apps.

Installing Sencha Cmd

Another optional component that can be installed is Sencha Cmd, which consists of command line tools that can be used to create and update Sencha Touch applications from a terminal.

The Sencha Cmd distribution can be downloaded from the same official download page of Sencha Touch (*http://www.sencha.com/products/touch/download/*). It requires a working Java installation in your workstation.

 At the time of this writing, the current version of Sencha Cmd was version 3.0.0.250.

After downloading Sencha Cmd, unzip the distribution file and execute the installer; Figure 1-1 shows the installer for OS X.

Figure 1-1. Sencha Cmd Installer

After you have installed the Sencha Cmd tools, make sure to update your PATH variable to point to the default location where the Sencha Cmd tools are installed:

```
~/bin/Sencha/Cmd/3.0.0.250
```

Mountain Lion and Java

The latest version of OS X at the time of this writing, Mountain Lion, does not include a Java Runtime Environment by default, and the Sencha Cmd Tools installer requires one to execute. You can force the installation of the latest JRE very easily by running `java -version` on a command line; this will prompt OS X to download and install it.

To make sure the installation went well, open a terminal window and type the `sencha` command; you should see an output similar to the following:

```
Sencha Cmd v3.0.0.250

Options
    * --debug, -d - Sets log level to higher verbosity
    * --plain, -p - enables plain logging output (no highlighting)
    * --quiet, -q - Sets log level to warnings and errors only
```

```
        * --sdk-path, -s - sets the path to the target framework

    Categories
        * app - Perform various application build processes
        * compile - Compile sources to produce concatenated output and metadata
        * fs - A set of useful utility actions to work with files.
        * generate - Generates models, controllers, etc. or an entire application
        * manifest - Extract class metadata
        * package - Packages a Sencha Touch application for native app stores
        * theme - Builds a set of theme images from a given html page

    Commands
        * ant - Invoke Ant with helpful properties back to Sencha Command
        * build - Builds a project from a JSB3 file.
        * config - Loads a config file or sets a configuration property
        * help - Displays help for commands
        * js - Executes arbitrary JavaScript file(s)
        * which - Displays the path to the current version of Sencha Cmd
```

We are going to use this tool later in this chapter; for the moment, let us see how to create a new application manually.

Creating a New Application

We are going to start our journey of discovery of Sencha Touch by creating the simplest possible application that you could create with it: a canonical "Hello, World!" application. It will have the following features:

- It will include all the required icons and default images supported by iOS and Android.
- It will use the most minimal *index.html* file possible.

Bare-Bones App

The most basic Sencha Touch application consists, at least, of the following:

1. The Sencha Touch libraries (which we have downloaded in the previous section)
2. An *index.html* file
3. One JavaScript file containing the source code of your application, which we will usually refer to in this book as *app.js*

Let's begin with *index.html*:

```
<!DOCTYPE html>
<html>
<head>
    <meta charset="utf-8" />
    <title>Hello World</title>

    <!-- Load Sencha Touch -->
    <link rel="stylesheet" href="/_libs/sencha/resources/css/
sencha-touch.css" />
    <script src="/_libs/sencha/sencha-touch-all-debug.js"></script>

    <!-- Load our code -->
    <script src="app.js"></script>
</head>
<body>
</body>
</html>
```

As you can see, this is the most bare-bones HTML5 file you could expect; it just specifies the encoding of the page, its title, and loads both the JavaScript and the CSS included in the Sencha Touch distribution. Finally, we load our own *app.js* JavaScript file, where the fun happens.

Do not forget the <body> tag!

Do not forget to add an opening and closing set of <body></body> tags, as otherwise your application might not appear on the screen. Sencha Touch manipulates the root element of the body tag to generate the required tags for the UI to appear on the screen.

Let's see now how the JavaScript file must be:

```
Ext.application({
    name: 'HelloWorld',
    launch: function () {
        // This is where the fun starts!
    }
});
```

At this stage, if you navigate to your file index.html using Safari or Chrome, you will be able to see an empty screen appear. If you use the web inspector provided by those browsers, you should not have any errors or warnings displayed. Not the best feedback, but we are going to add more personality to our application soon.

The Ext.application() Function

Every Sencha Touch application has at least the structure shown above, starting with the most important element, a call to the `Ext.application()` function, which takes a literal object as parameter.

This is a very common idiom in Sencha Touch; many functions are built in such a way that the developer has to pass only a literal object, usually also referred to as a dictionary, as the only parameter. We are going to see this pattern all over the framework:

```
Ext.someFunction({
    parameter1: 'value1',
    parameter2: false
});
```

The following technique will help you avoid typing errors or problems with unfinished dictionaries:

1. First, write the function signature in its entirety, without any parameters inside the brackets:

   ```
   Ext.someFunction({}); // yes, including the semicolon
   ```

2. Second, "open up" the curly brackets and fill the parameters inside:

   ```
   Ext.someFunction({ /* enter the parameters now */ });
   ```

Commas vs. semicolons

Remember that inside the curly brackets, the parameters are separated by commas, and not by semicolons. Using a "JavaScript Lint" tool in your editor will allow you to catch these and other common typing errors every time you save the file.

The call to the `Ext.application()` function takes as its sole parameter an object with two very important keys:

- `name`: This property is of type string and provides the root namespace for all the objects contained inside the application. Sencha Touch creates this namespace automatically for the developer, and this name will be used throughout the application to scope all objects and avoid cluttering the global namespace.

- `launch`: This property expects a function that will be executed when the framework code has been loaded and the application is ready to execute.

For all practical purposes, the `launch` function is the de facto entry point of your application; it is the location where the developer starts writing his own code, and begins providing personality and style to the app. For example, the following application will display an alert window when the application starts:

```
Ext.application({
    name: 'HelloWorld',
    launch: function () {
        Ext.Msg.alert('Application launched');
    }
});
```

You can see the result of the code in Figure 1-2.

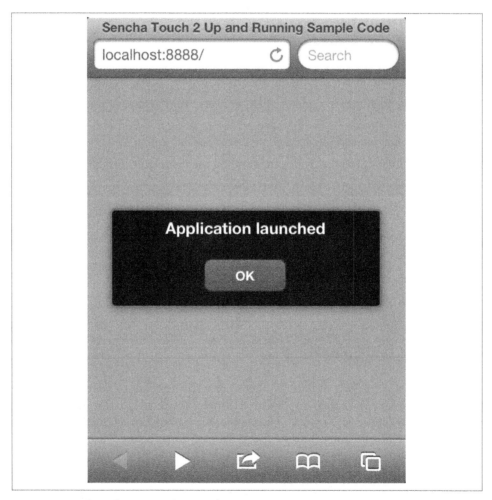

Figure 1-2. A bare-bones Sencha Touch 2 application

iOS developers might find it useful to think about the object passed as parameter of the Ext.application() function as the "application delegate" that is so common in the mobile operating system created by Apple.

What other parameters can be passed to the Ext.application() function? There are many of them, as shown in the following snippet:

```
Ext.application({
    name: 'HelloWorld',
    appFolder: 'app',
    profiles: ['Phone', 'Tablet', 'Desktop'],

    icon: {
        57: 'img/Icon.png',
        72: 'img/Icon-iPad.png',
        114: 'img/Icon@2x.png',       // Retina iPhone
        144: 'img/Icon-iPad@2x.png' // Retina iPad
    },

    startupImage: {
        '320x460': 'img/Default.png',
        '640x920': 'img/Default@2x.png', // Retina iPhone
        '768x1004': 'img/Default-Portrait.png',
        '748x1024': 'img/Default-Landscape.png',
        '1536x2008': 'img/Default-Portrait@2x.png', // Retina iPad, Portrait
        '1496x2048': 'img/Default-Landscape@2x.png' // Retina iPad, Landscape
    },

    models: [],
    views: [],
    controllers: [],

    fullscreen: true,
    isIconPrecomposed: true,
    statusBarStyle: 'black', // can also be 'default'

    launch: function () {
        Ext.Msg.alert('Application launched');
    }
});
```

- appFolder specifies an alternative location for the files of the application; by default, Sencha Touch loads automatically, on demand, the files located in an app folder, at the same level as the index.html file.

- profiles allows the application to become "universal," that is, to feature different user interfaces (UIs) for different supports. Sencha Touch supports three different profiles, for phones, tablets, and desktop browsers. Using profiles, a developer can create customized UIs for different devices, sharing the same controllers and low-level logic. Profiles are explained in detail in Chapter 10.

- `icon` takes a dictionary of number-string pairs; the number represents the size in pixels of the expected icon, and the string attached to the number is the relative location of the associated icon file.

- `startupImage` takes a dictionary as parameter, with keys representing the widths and heights of different iOS devices. The values of this dictionary are the paths to the corresponding startup images shown by iOS when the user opens a web application saved on the home screen.

- `models`, `views`, and `controllers` hold arrays of class names to be loaded automatically by Sencha Touch.

- `isIconPrecomposed` specifies whether the icon of the application, when saved on the home screen of an iOS device, receives the typical shading provided by the operating system.

- Finally, `statusBarStyle` specifies the type of status bar (black, default, or translucent) to be shown on top of the application when running on an iPhone or an iPod Touch device.

Using the information in the keys above, such as `icon` and `startupImage`, Sencha Touch generates the required `<meta>` tags in the DOM of the browser, as shown in Figure 1-3.

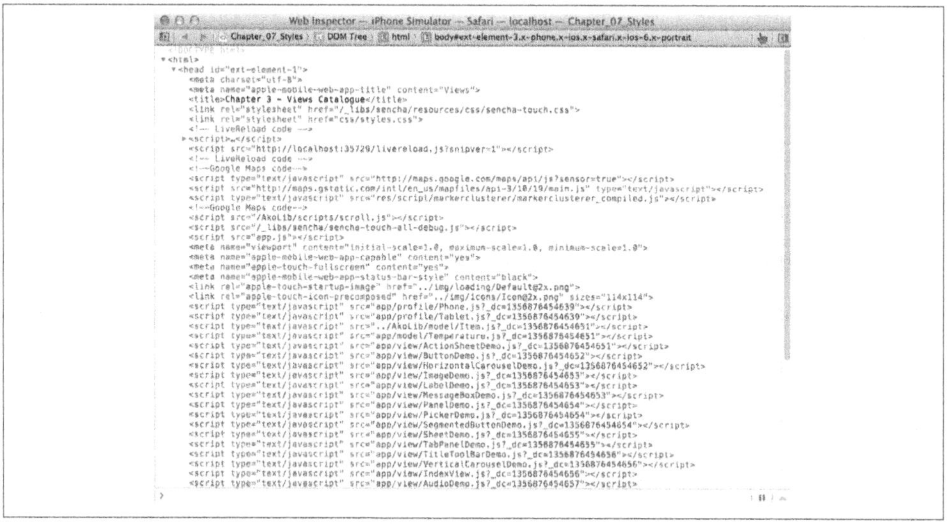

Figure 1-3. HTML5 meta tags generated by Sencha Touch 2

Using Sencha Cmd

Let us see now how to create a simple Sencha Touch application using the command-line tools.

 This section requires you to have the Sencha Cmd tools installed. Please refer to "Installing Sencha Cmd" (page 7) for more information.

The first thing to do is to open a terminal window and, assuming that the Sencha Touch folder is located inside the _libs folder (as is the case for the source code of this book), type the following command:

```
$ sencha -sdk _libs/sencha generate app NewApp ./NewAppFolder
```

The sencha generate app command takes two parameters: the name of the app (in this case NewApp) and the location (in this case, the NewAppFolder, which is a subfolder of the current location). The -sdk switch specifies the location (anywhere in the disk) of the Sencha Touch distribution (namely, the folder created when the ZIP file is unzipped.)

The terminal window will show the following output (edited for brevity):

```
Sencha Cmd v3.0.0.250
[INF]           init-properties:
[INF]           init-sencha-command:
[INF]           init:
[INF]           -before-generate-workspace:
[INF]           generate-workspace-impl:
[WRN]           Ignoring @require ../version/Version.js in js/String.js
[WRN]           Ignoring @require ../Ext-more.js in js/Format.js
[INF]           -before-copy-framework-to-workspace:
[INF]           copy-framework-to-workspace-impl:
[INF]               [copy] Copying 1103 files to NewApp/touch
[INF]                [copy] Copied 171 empty directories to 1 empty directory
under NewApp/touch
[INF]           [copy] Copying 1 file to NewApp/touch
[INF]           [copy] Copying 1 file to NewApp/touch
[INF]           [propertyfile] Updating property file: NewApp/.sencha/workspace/
sencha.cfg
    [...SNIP...]
[INF]           generate-app:
```

Finally, if you open your browser and navigate to the web application that has just been generated, you will see an output similar to that of Figure 1-4.

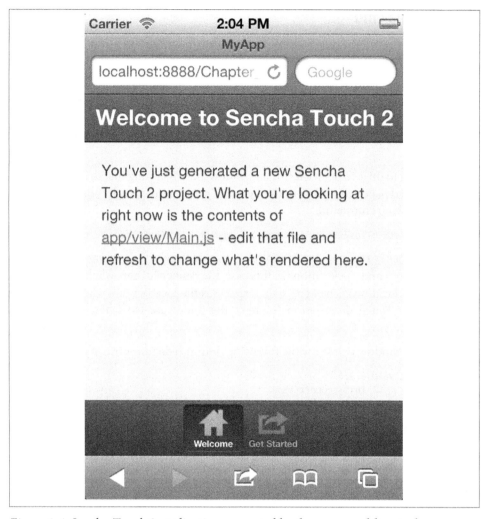

Figure 1-4. Sencha Touch 2 application generated by the command-line tools

 As mentioned in the preface of this book, please be aware that Sencha Touch applications use the XMLHTTPRequest object extensively and that opening your HTML files directly (that is, using the file:/// protocol) does not work; you should use a local web server instead.

Sencha Cmd provides many other services, which we will see in detail in Chapter 10. For the moment, suffice to say that the sencha command builds an application that conforms to the MVC standard enforced by Sencha Touch.

Overview of the Class Library

Sencha Touch comes bundled with a long list of components, objects, functions, and code ready to use out of the box. This class library is comparable with the ones bundled with the Java or .NET runtimes, and provides nearly all the basic blocks to create complex applications rapidly.

Not only that, but these classes are also built upon the principle of the MVC architecture, each of them fitting in a particular layer of a more complex architecture.

The Sencha Touch 2 class library includes the following families of classes:

- **Model classes**, providing developers with the means of describing the business entities that are ultimately managed, created, edited, and destroyed by your own applications. These classes are described independently of the storage medium required, be it remote or local, based upon JSON or XML. Chapter 4 provides more information about this subject.

- **Communication classes**, describing both the storage and communication strategies to be used when creating new applications. The most important classes in this family are Store, Proxy, and Reader, which provide common abstractions allowing applications to consume data from remote web services or to store information locally on the host browser.

- **Views**, which are used to easily build the user interface of any application with a consistent set of patterns; these are the most visible parts of the application and can use the advanced hardware acceleration capabilities of modern mobile devices to render themselves as quickly as possible, using CSS exclusively. Chapter 3 describes this family of classes in detail, showing examples of how to use the most important view components in your applications.

- **Controller classes** provide the glue between views and models, centralizing all the interaction in specialized classes, which hold the most important parts of the logic of the application. Controllers allow developers to organize their code in useful and reusable components, separating the business logic from the UI, and providing a more maintainable architecture for applications. Chapter 6 dives into this family in detail, showing all the advantages of using controllers in your own applications.

- **Utility classes** are pervasive in the framework and provide a tremendous amount of ready-to-use code, ranging from date and number formatters, containers, proxies, and many other classes.

The following chapters will deal with each of these families in detail.

Embedding Components

The usual data structure used to represent the in-memory structure of objects embedded into a user interface is the tree; this is very easy to achieve in Sencha Touch, thanks to one of the most important properties of any visual component: the items property.

The items property (available in subclasses of the Ext.Container class) takes an array of widgets ready to be embedded as children to the current component. For example:

```
Ext.define('BookApp.view.CustomList', {
    extend: 'Ext.dataview.List',

    config: {

        items: [{
            xtype: 'toolbar',
            title: 'To Do List',
            items: [{
                xtype: 'spacer'
            }, {
                xtype: 'button',
                iconCls: 'add',
                ui: 'plain'
            }]
        }]
    }
});
```

Analogies with other mobile platforms
For iOS developers, you can think of the items property as the Sencha Touch equivalent of the addSubview: method. In the case of Android, the equivalent API would be the addView() method of the View class. The biggest difference in the case of Sencha Touch is that the items property takes an array of views as parameter, while the APIs of both iOS and Android take individual view instances as parameters.

Layouts

However, a basic question remains: How does the parent component know how to embed the children component, particularly regarding its location on the screen? It turns out that many components are actually expected to be located in precise parts of the screen, like toolbars or navigation bars; in those cases, the component will be displayed exactly at the required location, without requiring further intervention from the developer.

For most components, however, it is required to specify the location of the child component in its parent; in those cases, you can add a layout parameter to the parent view, and then Sencha Touch will position the child objects accordingly to their respective orders in the `items` array.

Layouts will be described in great detail in Chapter 3.

Intro to Events

Most Sencha Touch user interface components are able to react to user events, and developers can attach functions to be executed every time one of these events is triggered.

It is very simple to attach functions as event handlers: The only thing that is required is to specify a `listeners` configuration element to your user interface object.

```
Ext.Viewport.add({
    xtype: 'panel',
    items: [{
        xtype: 'toolbar',
        docked: 'top',
        items: [{
            xtype: 'button',
            text: 'Show alert',
            listeners: {
                tap: function(button, e, eOpts) {
                    Ext.Msg.alert('Event triggered');
                }
            }
        }]
    }]
});
```

In the example above, the button in the toolbar is able to react to the `tap` event, which is one of the simplest events found in Sencha Touch. This event triggers the execution of the corresponding function, which takes a certain number of parameters; the Sencha Touch documentation, described in the next section, provides the exact definition of the parameters required in every one of the events exposed by the framework. Events will be described in more detail in Chapter 3.

However, attaching event handlers to view components using this approach can quickly lead to unmaintainable and/or non-reusable code, which somehow breaks the MVC architecture, as the business logic is intertwined with the view logic. Sencha Touch allows developers to centralize business logic and event handlers in controller classes, inheriting from `Ext.app.Controller`. This approach will be explained in Chapter 6.

Sencha Touch Documentation System

As mentioned before, the Sencha Touch distribution contains the entire API documentation that is available on the website; this makes it very easy to use and to refer to by developers, who can access this invaluable information even when offline. To open it, just double-click the docs/index.html file in your Sencha Touch distribution folder; Figure 1-5 shows the contents of the documentation when they are opened for the first time.

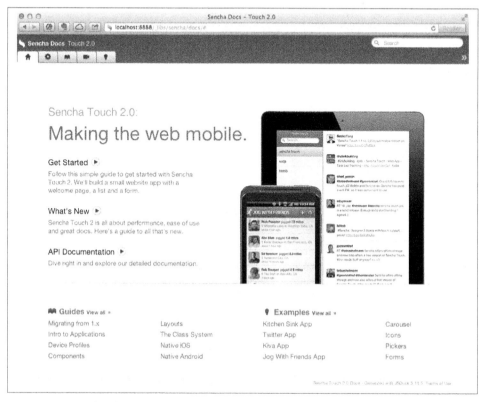

Figure 1-5. Sencha documentation system

The Sencha Touch documentation is bundled as an HTML5 application that uses the local storage of your browser to remember which tabs were open during your last session. This way, you will always find your way and, should you inadvertently close the browser window, the same pages will be opened for you the next time you access the documentation, as shown in Figure 1-6.

Figure 1-6. Sencha documentation tabs

Another handy feature of the built-in documentation system is integrated, full-text client-side search; type any text on the search field on the top right of the documentation browser, and you will be able to find your way. You can type any kind of API, function, even xtypes; all of them are just a keystroke away. Figure 1-7 shows how this brilliant search system works.

Figure 1-7. Sencha documentation search

It's a good idea to have this documentation system open at all times, whenever you are writing your Sencha Touch applications; the amount of information contained in it is invaluable. Even better, as we will learn in Chapter 8, you can generate the same kind of documentation for your own projects!

Conclusion

This chapter has shown you how to download the Sencha Touch distribution, and how to write and understand the basic principles of every application created with the framework. The next chapters will explore in depth different aspects of Sencha Touch, used to create very complex applications.

## CHAPTER 2

The Class System

This chapter will provide an overview of the most important central characteristic of Sencha Touch; the class system. This framework provides a higher-level object-oriented abstraction on top of JavaScript, allowing developers to define classes and to create instances using a syntax similar to that of other programming languages.

Although many JavaScript fans might find this approach heretical, the truth is that the class system provides a useful abstraction, helping developers achieve a higher productivity, creating more maintainable code.

This chapter ends with a discussion of the various extensions provided by Sencha Touch around the JavaScript core language and APIs, making developers write better cross-browser compatible code.

Architectural Considerations

Since its inception in the '70s, as part of the Smalltalk programming language, the MVC architecture has known many different interpretations. Every object-oriented framework or toolkit has brought its own flavor of MVC, sometimes inconsistent with other systems. It's enough to remember that Cocoa, Ruby on Rails, or Django, not to mention ASP.NET MVC, all propose slight variations of the MVC theme. These variations show the infinite flexibility of software, and the adaptability of design patterns to different situations and environments.

Sencha Touch is no different, as it provides yet another form of MVC, this time adapted to applications running on mobile web browsers. Figure 2-1 shows the typical structure of Sencha Touch MVC applications, which includes several new structural components:

- **Stores** are abstractions over arrays of model instances; data-bound components connect to stores to display lists or trees of data, delegating the sorting, ordering, and grouping of the data to the store. Data-bound views are tied to stores in such a way that any change to the data of the store will be updated automatically on the UI.

- **Proxies** are abstract entities that encapsulate the connection to a particular storage mechanism, either local or remote. Ideally, Sencha Touch applications are completely oblivious to the fact that the data is stored locally or remotely; stores use proxies to isolate the rest of the application from the underlying location of the data.

Both stores and proxies are explained in detail in Chapter 4.

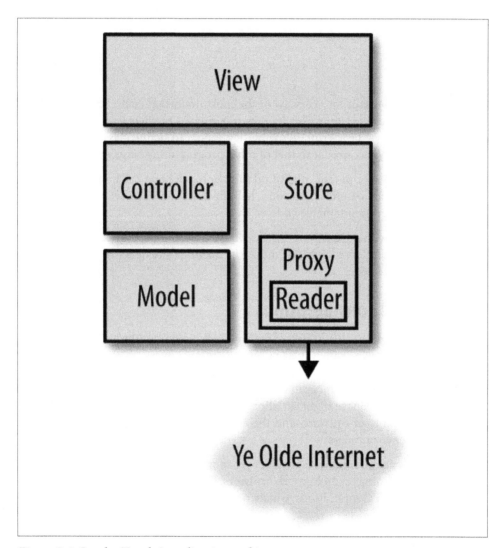

Figure 2-1. Sencha Touch 2 application architecture

Folder Organization

Sencha Touch MVC applications have a well-defined folder structure that is enforced throughout the framework, the class loader, Sencha Architect (explained in detail in Chapter 9) and even Sencha Cmd (explained in Chapter 10).

As you saw in Chapter 1, the code of your applications is contained within the app folder, located next to the *index.html* and *app.js* files. If for some reason you need to override this default location, the app.js file can contain an optional appFolder key, which will be used by the class loader instead.

Inside the app folder, the application code is structured as follows:

- controller contains all the classes specified in the controllers key of the Ext.application() function call in *app.js*.
- model contains the data model definitions.
- profile is where the different application profiles are stored.
- store contains the store definitions.
- Finally view is the placeholder for all the custom visual components used in the application.

Singular and plural names
Pay attention to the fact that folder names are singular words—app/controller, app/model, app/view—while the keys in the profiles or the Ext.application() function call in *app.js* are words in plural—controllers: [], models: [], views: [], and so on.

Understanding the Class System

JavaScript is a rather strange language, somewhat challenging to understand for developers used to more "traditional" programming languages such as Java, C#, or PHP. JavaScript has been defined by Douglas Crockford as "Lisp in C's clothing," and this description is actually very accurate, for JavaScript is a functional language; it is probably the most widely deployed and used functional programming language in the history of computing.

JavaScript also has some object-oriented features baked in, most of them being based on the functional nature of the language; JavaScript even has a "new" keyword, which leads developers to think that the class system is similar to that of Java or C++.

The reality sinks in quite fast, though; JavaScript does not have classes, at least not in the traditional sense of the word, but simply function templates that create in-memory structures linked to one another. JavaScript has only literal objects and functions; and with those two building blocks, you will create all of your web applications.

Sencha Touch tries to simplify and hide the quirkiest parts of JavaScript by providing its own class system; this makes it possible for developers to think about JavaScript in more traditional ways, defining classes and creating new instances from those.

As such, the Sencha Touch class system is based upon two main functions:

- `Ext.define()` allows developers to define a new class, including all its configuration options, static members, instance methods, event handlers, and other pieces.

- `Ext.create()` allows developers to create new instances of a class, overriding the default configuration options and providing useful run-time information.

 Both `Ext.define()` and `Ext.create()` are aliases of `Ext.ClassManag er.define()` and `Ext.ClassManager.instantiate()`, respectively. However, the latter methods are considered private, and you should always use the shorthand functions instead.

Let's define and create a simple class to see how all these elements work together.

```
Ext.define('BookApp.view.CustomList', {
    extend: 'Ext.dataview.List',
    xtype: 'customlist',
    config: {
        // ...
    }
});
```

In the preceding code, we define a new class called `BookApp.view.CustomList`; this class extends the `Ext.dataview.List` class and provides a custom `xtype` property as well; we'll see in the next section how to use this property.

 Classes defined using `Ext.define()` always ultimately inherit from `Ext.Base`, as do all the classes in the `Ext` namespace.

`Ext.Base` is not the same as `Ext.Class`, which is a class factory used internally by `Ext.ClassManager`, and which should not be accessed directly by developers.

Finally, a `config` parameter provides customization options that will be used to customize each new instance of this class during the lifetime of the application.

Now let's see how to create a new instance of the class we've just created:

```
var list = Ext.create('BookApp.view.CustomList');

// Alternatively you can also use the syntax below:
// var list = Ext.widget('customlist');
```

The preceding single statement is enough to get a pointer to a new instance of the
BookApp.view.CustomList class, which is exactly what we wanted to do here. If you
need to provide some extra configuration, just add a second parameter to the call to
Ext.create():

```
var list = Ext.create('BookApp.view.CustomList', {
    items: [
        // ...
    ],
    title: 'Some title',

    // ... more parameters here, separated by commas
});
```

Using xtypes

One of the most characteristic elements of the Sencha Touch 2 class system is the xtype
property. This property has a special meaning to Sencha Touch, and it represents a
mapping between a class name and a shorter name, easier to type and remember. In
short, you can think of the xtype as an alias to the real name of a class in the Sencha
Touch class system.

Thanks to the xtype property, Sencha Touch objects can be instantiated both with the
Ext.create() function, which requires the class name of the object, or by using dictionaries with the xtype keyword. When reading this parameter, Sencha Touch will
automatically create the object of the corresponding class. Alternatively, the Ext.widg
et() function can also be used to create objects just by specifying their xtype.

The following table shows the xtype values of different classes available in Sencha
Touch.

Table 2-1. Various xtypes already defined by Sencha Touch

Category	xtype	Class
Basic	button	Ext.Button
	component	Ext.Component
	container	Ext.Container
	dataview	Ext.DataView
	panel	Ext.Panel
	toolbar	Ext.Toolbar
	spacer	Ext.Spacer

Category	xtype	Class
	tabpanel	Ext.TabPanel
Form	form	Ext.form.FormPanel
	checkbox	Ext.form.Checkbox
	select	Ext.form.Select
	field	Ext.form.Field
	fieldset	Ext.form.FieldSet
	hidden	Ext.form.Hidden
	numberfield	Ext.form.NumberField
	radio	Ext.form.Radio
	slider	Ext.form.Slider
	textarea	Ext.form.TextArea
	textfield	Ext.form.TextField
Data	store	Ext.data.Store
	arraystore	Ext.data.ArrayStore
	jsonstore	Ext.data.JsonStore
	xmlstore	Ext.data.XmlStore

To use the xtype syntax, just create a standard JavaScript dictionary and use it in the items property of your panel, just as you would use any other instance.

```
Ext.define('BookApp.view.CustomList', {
    extend: 'Ext.dataview.List',
    config: {
        items: [{
            xtype: 'toolbar',
            title: 'To Do List',
            items: [{
                xtype: 'spacer'
            }, {
                xtype: 'button',
                iconCls: 'add',
                ui: 'plain'
            }]
        }]
    }
});
```

When Sencha Touch finds the preceding code, it will create a toolbar with a spacer and a button inside, automatically.

Overview of the Class Library

Sencha Touch comes bundled with a long list of components ready to use out of the box. This class library is comparable with the ones bundled with the Java or .NET runtimes, and provide nearly all the basic blocks to create complex applications rapidly.

Not only that, but these classes are also built upon the principle of the MVC architecture, each of them fitting in a particular layer of a more complex architecture.

The Sencha Touch 2 class library includes the following families of classes:

- **Model classes**, providing developers with the means of describing the business entities that are ultimately managed, created, edited, and destroyed by their applications. These classes are described independently of the storage medium required, be it remote or local, based upon JSON or XML. Chapter 4 provides more information about this subject.

- **Communication classes**, describing both the storage and communication strategies to be used when creating new applications. The most important classes in this family are the Store, Proxy, and Reader classes, which provide common abstractions allowing applications to consume data from remote web services, or to store information locally on the host browser. These components are also described in detail in Chapter 4.

- **Views**, which are used to describe the user interface of any application with ease and with a consistent set of patterns; these are the most visible parts of the application and can use the advanced hardware acceleration capabilities of modern mobile devices to render themselves as quickly as possible, using CSS exclusively. Chapter 3 describes this family of classes in detail, showing examples of how to use the most important view components in your applications.

- **Controller classes** provide the glue between views and models, centralizing all the interaction in specialized classes, which hold the most important parts of the logic of the application. Controllers allow developers to organize their code in useful and reusable components, separating the business logic from the UI, and providing a more maintainable architecture for applications. Chapter 6 dives into this family in detail, showing all the advantages of using controllers in your own applications.

- **Foundation utilities** are pervasive in the framework and provide a tremendous amount of ready-to-use code, ranging from date and number formatters, containers, proxies, and many other classes.

The following chapters will deal with every one of these families in detail; we are going to start our exploration with the foundation utilities family, which is used throughout the framework.

Foundation Utilities

As a convenience to developers, and to remove the requirement of using other JavaScript libraries (such as jQuery, Backbone.js, or Require.js), Sencha Touch provides an extensive foundation of functions and classes ready to be used. This section contains a summary of the most important functions available in Sencha Touch; for a complete description of each API, please refer to the documentation.

Ext

The Ext root object (also used as root namespace by Sencha Touch) contains a large number of useful functions and properties.

emptyFn

Ext.emptyFn contains a reusable, empty function that you can pass as a default parameter to callbacks or event handlers.

version

Ext.version returns the version of the current Sencha Touch library loaded in the browser.

application()

Ext.application(), described in detail in Chapter 1, is used to bootstrap the application during launch.

bind()

Ext.bind() is used to attach functions to objects, setting the correct this pointer at the end of the operation. This function is required to solve some quirks inherent to JavaScript.

clone()

Ext.clone() can be used to create a shallow copy of the object passed as parameter.

create(), define(), and widget()

Ext.define() is a shortcut for Ext.ClassManager.define() and is used to create new classes, as described earlier in this chapter. Similarly, Ext.create() is a shortcut to Ext.ClassManager.instantiate(), and is used to create new instances of the class whose name is passed as parameter. Finally, Ext.widget() can be used to create instances just by using the xtype instead of the whole class name.

decode() and encode()

Ext.decode() is a shortcut to Ext.JSON.decode(), used to parse a JSON string and return the corresponding object. Similarly, Ext.encode() is a shorthand for Ext.JSON.encode() and returns the JSON string that represents the object passed as parameter.

defer()

Ext.defer() is a shortcut for Ext.Function.defer(), used to delay the execution of a function by some milliseconds. The function also takes as parameters the context of execution, some optional arguments, and of course the number of milliseconds before executing the function. For more control over delayed execution, check the Ext.DelayedTask class, which provides tighter control and more options.

 Please refer to the section about Ext.Function.defer() that follows for more information and an example of use.

destroy()

Ext.destroy() is used to remove objects from memory completely, avoiding memory leaks or dangling references. The objects passed as parameters of this function will be removed from the DOM, and their event listeners will be removed as well.

each()

Ext.each() is a shortcut to Ext.Array.each(), and as the name implies, it takes an array as both parameter and function, and executes the function passing each element of the array as parameter. The callback function can be return false at any time to stop the iteration process.

getBody(), getDoc(), and getHead()

These three functions return a pointer to the current HTML elements representing the <body>, <html>, and <head> elements, respectively.

getClass() and getClassName()

These functions can be used to query any Sencha Touch object about itsclass:

```
var button = Ext.create('Ext.Button');
var classObject = Ext.getClass(button);
var className = Ext.getClassName(button);
```

The output of the Ext.getClass() function is a complex object dump, showing the complete internal structure of class objects:

```
$className: "Ext.Button"
$isClass: true
$onExtended: Array[2]
addConfig: function (config, fullMerge) {
addInheritableStatics: function (members) {
addMember: function (name, member) {
addMembers: function (members) {
addStatics: function (members) {
addXtype: function (xtype) {
arguments: null
borrow: function (fromClass, members) {
callParent: function (args) {
caller: null
create: function () {
createAlias: function (a, b) {
displayName: "Ext.Button"
extend: function (parent) {
getName: function () {
implement: function () {
length: 0
mixin: function (name, mixinClass) {
name: ""
onExtended: function (fn, scope) {
override: function (members) {
prototype: Object
superclass: Object
triggerExtended: function () {
xtype: "button"
__proto__: function Empty() {}
```

As expected, `Ext.getClassName()` has a simpler output: `Ext.Button`.

getCmp() and getStore()

These functions return pointers to specific Sencha Touch objects; `getCmp()` takes an ID as a parameter and returns a pointer to the corresponding component (not HTML element, but component!). On the other hand, `getStore()` is a shortcut to `Ext.da ta.StoreManager.lookup()` and provides a handy mechanism to get a pointer to any store defined in the current application.

 Sencha components are explained in detail in Chapter 3, while stores are described in Chapter 4.

id()

The `id()` function is used to create unique ID values for individual components.

---

isArray(), isBoolean(), isDate(), isDefined(), isElement(), and others

The Ext object exposes a series of similar methods returning Boolean values, stating the type of the objects passed as parameter; these functions are the following:

- isArray()
- isBoolean()
- isDate()
- isDefined()
- isElement()
- isEmpty()
- isFunction()
- isIterable()
- isNumber()
- isNumeric()
- isObject()
- isPrimitive()
- isString()

The usage and semantics of these functions are trivial:

```
var array = [];
var bool = Ext.isArray(array);
```

iterate()

The Ext.iterate() function provides a unified interface that allows you to repeat a function over all the objects contained in arrays or objects, indistinctively:

```
var obj = {
    key1: 'value1',
    key2: 'value2',
    key3: 345,
    key4: false
};
Ext.iterate(obj, function (key, value) {
    var str = key + ': ' + value;
    console.log(str);
}, this);

var arr = [ 'value1', 'value2', 678, true ];
var index = 0;
Ext.iterate(arr, function (item) {
    var str = index + '> ' + item;
```

```
    console.log(str);
    ++index;
  }, this);
```

The function detects the type of object passed as parameter and executes the corresponding function in either Ext.Array or Ext.Object, as required. This is the output of the preceding code:

```
key1: value1
key2: value2
key3: 345
key4: false
0> value1
1> value2
2> 678
3> true
```

namespace()

The namespace() function (and its alias ns()) take a string literal with a namespace definition (usually a long list of strings separated by dots) and dynamically and recursively create the nested object structure that it represents. This is done immediately and synchronously, which means that the JavaScript code can reference those objects right after the namespace() function call.

```
Ext.namespace('Whatever.You.Want.Here.can.be.Done');
console.dir(Whatever);
```

The output would be an object whose structure is the following:

```
Object
    You: Object
        Want: Object
            Here: Object
                can: Object
                    be: Object
                        Done: Object
```

typeOf()

Similarly to the isArray() family of functions previously described, the typeOf() function works as an extended (and patched) alternative to the typeof() function provided by the JavaScript standard. The following code shows an example of how to use it:

```
var undef;
var nil = null;
var str = 'string';
var num = 234;
var bool = true;
var date = new Date();
var func = function () {
```

```
    console.log('something');
};
var obj = { key1: 'value1' };
var arr = [ 'value1', 'value2' ];
var reg = /match/gi;
var elem = Ext.getDoc().dom;

var all = [ undef, nil, str, num, bool, date, func, obj, arr, reg, elem ];

var index = 0;
Ext.iterate(all, function (item) {
    var txt = index + '> ' + item + ': ' + Ext.typeOf(item);
    console.log(txt);
    ++index;
}, this);
```

The result of the execution of this code is the following:

```
0> undefined: undefined
1> null: null
2> string: string
3> 234: number
4> true: boolean
5> Wed Nov 07 2012 14:24:22 GMT+0100 (CET): date
6> function () {
    console.log('something');
}: function
7> [object Object]: object
8> value1,value2: array
9> /match/gi: regexp
10> [object HTMLHtmlElement]: element
```

Ext.Array

The Ext.Array object contains a large number of utility functions that developers can use to manipulate arrays. They provide workarounds to solve common problems appearing in some implementations of JavaScript (such as in Internet Explorer), and they provide great value in very simple APIs.

These methods all work on top of the standard JavaScript Array class, but they are not instance methods; they are class methods. This approach has the benefit of not polluting the existing Array class with methods that could be implemented in future versions of the language, making your code stable in case of future evolutions.

clean()

The `clean()` function removes "empty" items from an array. The mentioned earlier empty in this case is brought by the `Ext.isEmpty()` function, described later in this chapter.

```
var sampleArray = [1234, true, 'asdfadf', null, 'another string', '', 0];
var cleanArray = Ext.Array.clean(sampleArray);
```

The preceding code yields an array that only contains the values [1234, true, 'asdfadf', 'another string', 0].

contains()

The `contains()` function returns a Boolean value stating whether a certain value exists in the array or not.

```
var sampleArray = [1234, true, 'asdfadf', null, 'another string', '', 0];
var tests = [false, '', 'whatever', 'asdfadf', 1234, 6578];

Ext.Array.each(tests, function (item) {
    if (Ext.Array.contains(sampleArray, item)) {
        console.log('"' + item + '" IS contained');
    }
    else {
        console.log('"' + item + '" is NOT contained');
    }
}, this);
```

The result of the code is the following:

```
"false" is NOT contained
"" IS contained
"whatever" is NOT contained
"asdfadf" IS contained
"1234" IS contained
"6578" is NOT contained
```

difference()

The `difference()` function returns a new array containing the result of subtracting, from the first array passed as parameter, the elements that exist in a second array passed as parameter. For example:

```
var sampleArray = [1234, true, 'asdfadf', null, 'another string', '', 0];
var anotherArray = ['asdfadf', new Date(), 1234, true, '', 234];
var difference = Ext.Array.difference(sampleArray, anotherArray);
```

The contents of the preceding `difference` variable are the following: [null, 'another string', 0].

erase()

The erase() function provides a simpler API to the standard Array.splice() method of the JavaScript standard library. It allows you to remove a certain number of items from an array, starting at a particular point.

```
var sampleArray = [1234, true, 'asdfadf', null, 'another string', '', 0];
var erasedArray = Ext.Array.erase(sampleArray, 1, 3);
```

The result of the preceding code is the following: [1234, 'another string', '', 0].

every() and some()

The every() and some() functions iterate over the items of an array, evaluating each of them in a function passed as parameter; both functions work very similarly, with the difference that every() stops iterating as soon as the function returns false, while some() will stop iterating as soon as the function returns true. For example:

```
var sampleArray = [1234, true, 'asdfadf', null, 'another string', '', 0];
var result = Ext.Array.every(sampleArray, function (item) {
    // If here the inner function returns "false" at any point, the
    // loop ends and the value in "result" will be "false."
    // In this case, however, as 'whatever' is not contained in the
    // sampleArray, the function always returns true, and 'result'
    // contains true as well.
    return (item !== 'whatever');
}, this);
console.log('Result of `every()`: ' + result);

var sampleArray = [1234, true, 'asdfadf', null, 'another string', '', 0];
console.log('Original Array');
console.dir(sampleArray);
var result = Ext.Array.some(sampleArray, function (item) {
    // If here the inner function returns "true" at any point, the
    // loop ends and the value in "result" will be "true."
    // In this case, however, as 'another string' is contained in the
    // sampleArray, the function returns true at some point, and 'result'
    // contains true as well.
    return (item === 'another string');
}, this);
console.log('Result of some(): ' + result);
```

The respective outputs would look like this:

```
Result of every(): true
Result of some(): true
```

The preceding results can be read as follows: "Every item in the first array was different from whatever," and "Some item in the second array was equal to another string."

filter()

The `filter()` function evaluates every item of the array passed as parameter, and it returns a new array that contains all the values where the provided function returns true.

```
var sampleArray = [1234, true, 'asdfadf', null, 'another string', '', 0];
var filteredArray = Ext.Array.filter(sampleArray, function (item) {
    return (typeof(item) === 'string');
}, this);
```

In the preceding code, the resulting array will contain only the strings: ['asdfadf', 'another string', ''].

flatten()

The `flatten()` function takes an array with nested arrays and brings all the values in the nested arrays as part of the topmost one:

```
var sampleArray = [1234, true, 'asdfadf', ['inner array', true, false, 234],
'another string', '', 0];
var flattenedArray = Ext.Array.flatten(sampleArray);
```

The result of the code is the following array: [1234, true, "asdfadf", "inner array", true, false, 234, "another string", "", 0].

from()

The `from()` function creates a new array from any object or primitive passed as parameter:

```
var bool = true;
var booleanArray = Ext.Array.from(bool);
```

The preceding code yields an array containing a single value inside: [true].

include()

The `include()` function works like a selective `push()` method: It adds new items to an array only if those items do not already exist, ensuring that the each element appears only once:

```
var sampleArray = [1234, 456, true, 'test'];
Ext.Array.include(sampleArray, true);
Ext.Array.include(sampleArray, 'whatever');
```

The result of the preceding code is the following array: [1234, 456, true, 'test', 'whatever']. The value `true` is not added a second time, since it already exists when the first call to `include()` is made.

indexOf()

As the name implies, this function returns the index of the item passed as parameter. In case the object is not found, the function returns -1:

```
var sampleArray = [1234, 456, true, 'test'];
var index = Ext.Array.indexOf(sampleArray, 'whatever');
console.log('Index of "whatever" (should be -1):');
```

insert()

The insert() function allows you to interpolate values in an existing array at a particular position:

```
var sampleArray = [1234, 456, true, 'test'];
var itemsToInsert = [768, 'something', false, null];
var insertedArray = Ext.Array.insert(sampleArray, 1, itemsToInsert);
```

The result of the preceding code is the following: [1234, 768, "something", false, null, 456, true, "test"]. The values of the array itemsToInsert have been embedded in the first array, starting at position number 1.

intersect()

The intersect() function returns a new array that merges the values from all the arrays passed as parameter (this function can take a large number of arguments):

```
var sampleArray = [1234, 456, true, 'test'];
var anotherArray = [true, false, 'test', 'whatever', 456];
var intersection = Ext.Array.intersect(anotherArray, sampleArray);
```

The result of the intersection is the following: [true].

map() and pluck()

The map() and pluck() functions will sound familiar to developers versed in functional languages such as Haskell or Lisp. They both operate over the contents of an array but in different ways: map() will execute a function in each item, returning a new array with the results of each execution. On the other hand, pluck() will return a new array with the values of a particular key from an array of objects:

```
var sampleArray = [1234, 456, true, 'test'];
var mapped = Ext.Array.map(sampleArray, function (item) {
    return item + '_boom';
}, this);
```

The mapped array looks like this: ['1234_boom', '456_boom', 'true_boom', 'test_boom'].

```
var sampleArray = [{
    key1: 'value1',
    key2: 'value2'
```

```
    }, {
        key1: 'value3',
        key2: 'value4'
    }, {
        key1: 'value5',
        key2: 'value6'
    }, {
        key1: 'value7',
        key2: 'value8'
    }, {
        key1: 'value9',
        key2: 'value0'
    }];
    console.log('Original Array');
    console.dir(sampleArray);
    var plucked = Ext.Array.pluck(sampleArray, 'key1');
```

After this code executes, `plucked` contains all the values referenced by the key `key1`:
`[ 'value1', 'value3', 'value5', 'value7', 'value9' ]`.

max(), mean(), min(), and sum()

All of these functions perform the typical mathematical operations on any array:

```
    var sampleArray = [1234, 456, -234, 654, 0, 'whatever'];
    var max = Ext.Array.max(sampleArray);
    var min = Ext.Array.min(sampleArray);
    var sum = Ext.Array.sum(sampleArray);

    var sampleArray2 = [1234, 456, -234, 654, 0];
    var mean = Ext.Array.mean(sampleArray2);
```

After executing the preceding code, `max` is 1234, `min` is equal to -234, `sum` is `2110what ever` (pay attention to how the string was added at the end of the mathematical sum!) and `mean` is equal to 422.

merge() and union()

The `merge()` function (and its alias `union()`) create a new array with all the values of those passed as parameter, but appearing only once:

```
    var sampleArray = [1234, 456, true, 'test'];
    var anotherArray = [true, false, 'test', 'whatever', 456];
    var merge = Ext.Array.merge(anotherArray, sampleArray);
```

The result of the preceding code is the following: `[ true, false, 'test', 'whatev er', 456, 1234 ]`.

remove()

The remove() function, as the name implies, removes items from an array, but only if they exist (of course!):

```
var sampleArray = [1234, 456, -234, 654, 0, 'whatever', "BOOM", true, 'test'];
Ext.Array.remove(sampleArray, 'whatever');
Ext.Array.remove(sampleArray, -234);
Ext.Array.remove(sampleArray, true);
Ext.Array.remove(sampleArray, 'non existent value');
```

The result of the code is that sampleArray now contains the values [1234, 456, 654, '0', 'BOOM', 'test'].

replace() and splice()

The replace() function takes two arrays as parameters and replaces values in the first array using the values in the second. For that it also requires some indexing information, in particular the location where to start making replacements in the first array, and the number of such replacements to make.

```
var sampleArray = [1234, 456, -234, 654, 0, 'whatever', "BOOM", true, 'test'];
var replacements = ['boom', 'boom again'];
Ext.Array.replace(sampleArray, 4, 2, replacements);
```

The result of the preceding code is the following: [1234, 456, -234, 654, "boom", "boom again", "BOOM", true, "test"]. As you can see, the values of the replace ments array was inserted after the fifth item, replacing the values 0 and whatever.

The splice() function does exactly the same; however, it uses the same signature of the function of the same name in the JavaScript standard library:

```
var sampleArray = [1234, 456, -234, 654, 0, 'whatever', "BOOM", true, 'test'];
Ext.Array.splice(sampleArray, 4, 2, 'boom', 'boom again');
```

The result of this code is exactly the same as the one returned by the replace() function.

slice()

The slice() function returns a subsection of an existing array, and it takes both the start and end indexes.

 A very common error when using this function is to consider the second argument to be the length of the requested slice; it is not a length, it is the ending index!

```
var sampleArray = [1234, 456, -234, 654, 0, 'whatever', "BOOM", true, 'test'];
var slice = Ext.Array.slice(sampleArray, 4, 7);
```

The result of this method is the following: [0, 'whatever', 'BOOM'].

sort()

The sort() function takes an array and a comparison function as parameter and returns a new array with the same items as the original one, but sorted:

```
var sampleArray = [1234, true, 'ASDFADF', -76, '', null, 'another string', '',
0];
var sorted = Ext.Array.sort(sampleArray, function (item1, item2) {
    if (item1 === item2) {
        return 0;
    }
    return (item1 < item2) ? -1 : 1;
});
```

The result of the code is the following: [-76, "", null, "", 0, true, 1234, "ASD FADF", "another string"].

toArray()

The toArray() function transforms an "iterable object" into a real array. This includes the arguments object (automatic object containing all the arguments of a function in JavaScript) as well as any literal object whose keys are numeric:

```
var iterable = {
    0: 'value0',
    1: 'value1',
    2: 'value2',
    3: 'value3',
    4: 'value4',
    length: 5
};
var array = Ext.Array.toArray(iterable);
```

The preceding code yields an array with these values: ['value0', 'value1', 'value2', 'value3', 'value4'].

unique()

The unique() function returns a new array with only one instance of each repeated object in the original array:

```
var sampleArray = [1234, 456, 'whatever', 'whatever', 456, 'whatever'];
var unique = Ext.Array.unique(sampleArray);
```

The result of this function call is the following: [1234, 456, 'whatever'].

Ext.ComponentQuery

The `Ext.ComponentQuery` singleton object provides a very useful `query()` function, used to retrieve pointers to one or many individual components in the application using a syntax similar to that of CSS selectors. This functionality is heavily used in Sencha Touch controllers (described in more detail in Chapter 6).

 Although very similar to `Ext.DomQuery`, the `Ext.Component Query.query()` function does not return pointers to DOM elements, but rather Sencha Touch components, themselves represented by one or many DOM elements. The results of `Ext.ComponentQuery` are then higher in the abstraction ladder.

Component Query Syntax

The component query syntax is very similar to that of CSS selectors; to retrieve components, you can use the following options:

- The `xtype` property.
- The `itemId` property, using the `#myItemId` syntax (just like in CSS).
- Attributes wrapped in brackets, such as `button[action=saveFile]`.
- Functions returning "truthy" values, using curly brackets: `{isHidden()}`.
- Optionally, you can use the `>` sign to indicate parent/child relationships, or the comma (`,`) to concatenate different queries in one: `panel > button`, or `button, segmentedbutton` are some examples.
- Finally, the not operator can also be used: `not button` will return all the components that are not buttons in the application.

Ext.DateExtras

Sencha Touch includes a series of utility methods for managing date and time information contained within the `Ext.DateExtras` object. These functions all work with the standard `Date` class provided by the standard JavaScript library.

Similarly to the `Ext.Array` functions, many of these functions do not exist as instance methods of the `Date` class, but rather as static methods of the `Ext.Date` object.

Pay attention to the fact that these functions are not included by default by Sencha Touch; to use them in your code, you have to include the following line in the controller or view where you wish to use them: `requires: 'Ext.DateExtras'`. However, to use them, you have to use the Ext.Date object.

add()

The `add()` function allows you to increment or decrement a given date by a certain interval. The type of interval can be specified using the constants available in the Ext.Date object, such as DAY, HOUR, or MONTH.

```
var sampleDate = new Date();
var futureDate = Ext.Date.add(sampleDate, Ext.Date.DAY, 10);
```

The result of this code is a date 10 days in the future.

between()

The `between()` function takes three dates and evaluates whether the first one is located amid the other two dates passed as parameters:

```
var sampleDate = new Date();
var anotherDate = Ext.Date.add(sampleDate, Ext.Date.YEAR, 10);
var betweenDate = Ext.Date.add(sampleDate, Ext.Date.MONTH, 5);
var inBetween = Ext.Date.between(betweenDate, sampleDate, anotherDate);
```

In this case, the inBetween variable contains the true value.

clearTime()

This useful function removes any time information from the date passed as parameter.

```
var sampleDate = new Date();
var noTime = Ext.Date.clearTime(sampleDate);
```

format()

This is probably one of the most useful additions of the Ext.DateExtras object: This function allows developers to display date and time information in human-readable form, using the same format specifiers known to PHP developers.

The specifiers accepted by the `format()` are described in the following table:

Table 2-2. Formats accepted by the format() function

Format	Examples	Description
d	01 to 31	Day of the month, two digits with leading zeros
D	Mon to Sun	A short textual representation of the day of the week

Format	Examples	Description
j	1 to 31	Day of the month without leading zeros
l	Sunday to Saturday	A full textual representation of the day of the week
N	1 (for Monday) through 7 (for Sunday)	ISO-8601 numeric representation of the day of the week
S	st, nd, rd or th. Works well with j.	English ordinal suffix for the day of the month, two characters
w	0 (for Sunday) to 6 (for Saturday)	Numeric representation of the day of the week
z	0 to 364 (365 in leap years)	The day of the year (starting from 0)
W	01 to 53	ISO-8601 week number of year, weeks starting on Monday
F	January to December	A full textual representation of a month, such as January or March
m	01 to 12	Numeric representation of a month, with leading zeros
M	Jan to Dec	A short textual representation of a month
n	1 to 12	Numeric representation of a month, without leading zeros
t	28 to 31	Number of days in the given month
L	1 if it is a leap year, 0 otherwise.	Whether it's a leap year
o	1998	ISO-8601 year number (identical to Y, but if the ISO week number [W] belongs to the previous or next year, then that year is used instead)
Y	1999	A full numeric representation of a year, four digits
y	03	A two-digit representation of a year
a	am or pm	Lowercase ante meridiem and post meridiem
A	AM or PM	Uppercase ante meridiem and post meridiem
g	1 to 12	12-hour format of an hour without leading zeros
G	0 to 23	24-hour format of an hour without leading zeros
h	01 to 12	12-hour format of an hour with leading zeros
H	00 to 23	24-hour format of an hour with leading zeros
i	00 to 59	Minutes, with leading zeros
s	00 to 59	Seconds, with leading zeros
u	999876543210	Decimal fraction of a second (minimum one digit, arbitrary number of digits allowed)
O	+1030	Difference to Greenwich Mean Time (GMT) in hours and minutes
P	-08:00	Difference to Greenwich Mean Time (GMT) with colon between hours and minutes
T	EST, MDT, PDT . . .	Time zone abbreviation of the machine running the code
Z	-43200 to 50400	Time zone offset in seconds (negative if west of UTC, positive if east)
c	1997-05-16T19:23:30,12345-0400	ISO-8601 date (see *http://www.w3.org/TR/NOTE-datetime* for more info)
U	1193432466 or -2138434463	Seconds since the Unix Epoch (January 1 1970 00:00:00 GMT)
MS	\/Date(1238606590509)\/	Microsoft AJAX serialized dates

The following code shows a simple usage example of the `format()` function:

```
var sampleDate = new Date();
var patterns = {
```

```
        ISO8601Long:"Y-m-d H:i:s",
        ISO8601Short:"Y-m-d",
        ShortDate: "n/j/Y",
        LongDate: "l, F d, Y",
        FullDateTime: "l, F d, Y g:i:s A",
        MonthDay: "F d",
        ShortTime: "g:i A",
        LongTime: "g:i:s A",
        SortableDateTime: "Y-m-d\\TH:i:s",
        UniversalSortableDateTime: "Y-m-d H:i:sO",
        YearMonth: "F, Y"
    };
    var key = null;
    var format = '';
    console.log('Formatted dates:');
    for (key in patterns) {
        if (patterns.hasOwnProperty(key)) {
            format = patterns[key];
            formatted = Ext.Date.format(sampleDate, format);
            console.log(format + ': ' + formatted);
        }
    }
```

The output of the code is the following:

```
Formatted dates:
Y-m-d H:i:s: "2012-11-07 11:06:24"
Y-m-d: "2012-11-07"
n/j/Y: "11/7/2012"
l, F d, Y: "Wednesday, November 07, 2012"
l, F d, Y g:i:s A: "Wednesday, November 07, 2012 11:06:24 AM"
F d: "November 07"
g:i A: "11:06 AM"
g:i:s A: "11:06:24 AM"
Y-m-d\TH:i:s: "2012-11-07T11:06:24"
Y-m-d H:i:sO: "2012-11-07 11:06:24+0100"
F, Y: "November, 2012"
```

getDayOfYear(), getWeekOfYear(), isLeapYear()

These functions provide useful information about the year of the date passed as parameter and are quite self-explanatory:

```
var sampleDate = new Date();

var dayOfYear = Ext.Date.getDayOfYear(sampleDate);
var week = Ext.Date.getWeekOfYear(sampleDate);
var isLeap = Ext.Date.isLeapYear(sampleDate);
```

getDaysInMonth(), getFirstDateOfMonth(), getFirstDayOfMonth(), getLastDateOfMonth(), getLastDayOfMonth()

These functions provide information about the month of the date passed as parameter:

```
var sampleDate = new Date();

var daysInMonth = Ext.Date.getDaysInMonth(sampleDate);

var firstDate = Ext.Date.getFirstDateOfMonth(sampleDate);
var firstDay = Ext.Date.getFirstDayOfMonth(sampleDate);
var firstDayName = Ext.Date.dayNames[firstDay];

var lastDate = Ext.Date.getLastDateOfMonth(sampleDate);
var lastDay = Ext.Date.getLastDayOfMonth(sampleDate);
var lastDayName = Ext.Date.dayNames[lastDay];
```

getElapsed()

The getElapsed() function returns the time interval in milliseconds between two dates passed as parameter:

```
var sampleDate = new Date();
var anotherDate = Ext.Date.add(sampleDate, Ext.Date.YEAR, 10);
var elapsed = Ext.Date.getElapsed(sampleDate, anotherDate);
```

The preceding code returns the value 315532800000, which is the number of milliseconds contained in a 10-year period.

getGMTOffset(), getTimezone(), isDST()

These functions provide information about the time zone of the date instance passed as a parameter:

```
var sampleDate = new Date();
var offset = Ext.Date.getGMTOffset(sampleDate);
var timezone = Ext.Date.getTimezone(sampleDate);
var isDST = Ext.Date.isDST(sampleDate);
```

At the moment of this writing, the values returned by these functions are as follows: +0100 for the offset, CET for the time zone, and false for the DST information.

getMonthNumber(), getShortDayName(), getShortMonthName(), getSuffix()

These functions are useful helpers for displaying time and date information in a human-readable way:

```
var number = Ext.Date.getMonthNumber("June");
var shortDayName = Ext.Date.getShortDayName(4);
var shortMonthName = Ext.Date.getShortMonthName(4);

var sampleDate = new Date();
var suffix = Ext.Date.getSuffix(sampleDate);
```

In the last case, at the moment of this writing the suffix returned is th, but of course it could be any value, such as st, nd, rd, or th.

isValid()

The isValid() function takes at least values for year, month, and day (in that order), optionally for time information and checks whether they correspond to valid date values. This might be handy when checking user input in forms, for example:

```
var isValid1 = Ext.Date.isValid(1984, 4, 6);
var isValid2 = Ext.Date.isValid(355423, 4564564, 23424);
```

As you can easily imagine, the first set of values yields a valid date, while the second does not.

parse()

Finally, the parse() function takes a string with date information and an optional format parameter and returns the Date instance that corresponds.

```
var parsed = Ext.Date.parse('2012-11-15', 'Y-m-d');
```

Ext.DomHelper and Ext.DomQuery

Sencha Touch also provides the required functionality for web developers to refer to the HTML elements that make up a web page, individually or as a group. For that, it exposes functions similar to those of jQuery or Zepto, taking very similar parameters and behaving in similar ways.

select() and selectNode()

Using select() and selectNode(), developers can retrieve pointers to individual HTML objects (or groups thereof) in the current context:

```
var divs = Ext.DomQuery.select('DIV');
var div = Ext.DomQuery.selectNode('#queryDiv');
```

The allowed element selectors are the following (in this example, we are using li and ul as an example, but any HTML tag can be used in this context):

*
> any element

ul, li
> an element with any of these tags

ul li
> all descendant li elements of ul

ul > li
> all li that are direct children of ul

ul + li

all li elements that are immediately preceded by ul

ul ~ li

all li elements that are preceded by a sibling element with the tag ul

 The use of quotes and the @ sign are optional in attribute selectors.

Developers can also use attribute selectors:

ul[class]

an ul element that has a class attribute

ul[class=main]

an ul element that has a class attribute with the main value

ul[class$=main]

an ul element that has a class attribute that ends with the main value

ul[class*=main]

an ul element that has a class attribute that contains the main value

ul[class%=2]

an ul element that has a class attribute whose value is evenly divisable by 2

ul[class!=main]

an ul element that has a class attribute that does not equal the main value

CSS value selectors are also possible and use the same syntax as attribute selectors but with curly brackets instead of square brackets: ul{display=block}, for example.

Finally, pseudo-class selectors are also possible: li:first-child, li:last-child, li:only-child, li:4th-child, li:odd, li:even, etc.

append(), insertBefore(), insertAfter(), overwrite(), insertHtml()

Once you have selected one or many nodes, Ext.DomHelper provides useful functions that allow you to manipulate the HTML nodes. For example, taking the following HTML fragment:

```
<div class="outerDiv"><div id="someDiv" class="innerDiv"></div></div>
```

We can operate on it as follows, and Figure 2-2 shows the result:

```
var div = Ext.DomQuery.selectNode('#someDiv');
```

```
Ext.DomHelper.overwrite(div, '<div id="someDiv">This is an overwritten DIV</
div>');
Ext.DomHelper.append(div, '<p>A paragraph added using append()</p>');
Ext.DomHelper.insertBefore(div, '<p>A paragraph inserted before the div</p>');
Ext.DomHelper.insertAfter(div, '<p>A paragraph inserted after the div</p>');

// Valid parameters:
// beforeBegin: <HERE><div>Contents</div>
// afterBegin: <div><HERE>Contents</div>
// beforeEnd: <div>Contents<HERE></div>
// afterEnd: <div>Contents</div><HERE>
Ext.DomHelper.insertHtml('beforeBegin', div, '<div class="inserted">inserted as
HTML</div>');
```

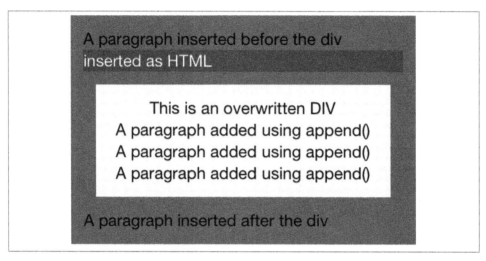

Figure 2-2. Ext.DomHelper manipulations

Ext.env.Feature

The `Ext.env.Feature` class (of which `Ext.feature` is the singleton instance) exposes a series of properties, each highlighting a particular HTML5 feature of the browser where the application is running:

```
var key = null;
var value = false;
var text = '';
console.log('Available features:');
for (key in Ext.feature.has) {
    value = Ext.feature.has[key];
    text = key + ': ' + value;
    console.log(text);
}
```

After executing this code in Safari 6.0.2 on OS X Mountain Lion, this is the result:

```
Available features:
Canvas: true
Svg: true
Vml: true
Touch: false
Orientation: false
OrientationChange: false
DeviceMotion: false
Geolocation: true
SqlDatabase: true
WebSockets: true
Range: true
CreateContextualFragment: true
History: true
CssTransforms: true
Css3dTransforms: true
CssAnimations: true
CssTransitions: true
Audio: true
Video: true
ClassList: true
LocalStorage: true
```

 Chapter 10 includes a description about how to access native device
functionality such as geolocation or orientation from Sencha Touch
applications.

Ext.Function

The Ext.Function object contains useful helper…well, functions, that extend and aug-
ment the already interesting native capabilities of JavaScript functions. Many of these
functions are used by Sencha Touch for managing event handling, supporting extended
events (such as double-tap events) and other features. They are also available for developers to use (and maybe abuse).

createDelayed()

The createDelayed() function wraps a function, causes a delay in milliseconds, and
returns a new function that fires the wrapped function after the requested delay:

```
var fn = function (value) {
    console.log('this is fn, this is the value: "' + value + '"');
};

var delayed = Ext.Function.createDelayed(fn, 1500, this, [ 345 ]);

delayed();
```

This function causes the text this is fn, this is the value: "345" on the console after approximately a second and a half.

createInterceptor()

The createInterceptor() function takes a function and wraps it with another one, composing everything into a third one that is returned. When this returned function is executed, all input is piped to the wrapping function (the second argument) which must return true or false. The original function (the wrapped one, passed as first argument) is executed only if the wrapper returns true.

In the following example, originalFn() is executed only when interceptor() is called with a value of 234; the check is performed by newFn().

```
var originalFn = function (value) {
    console.log('original function, this is the value: "' + value + '"');
};

var newFn = function (value) {
    console.log('inside newFn, value is "' + value + '"');
    return (value === 234);
};

var interceptor = Ext.Function.createInterceptor(originalFn, newFn);

interceptor(0);
interceptor(666);
interceptor(234);
```

The output of the code is the following:

```
inside newFn, value is "0"
inside newFn, value is "666"
inside newFn, value is "234"
this is the original function, this is the value: "234"
```

This mechanism is very useful to filter input to functions, composing them as required, on the fly, at runtime.

createSequence()

The createSequence() function is used to chain the execution of functions together; it takes two functions, and returns a new one. When the returned function is called, the wrapped functions are called, with their parameters passed accordingly. However, the return value of the wrapping function is the return value of the first function wrapped.

```
var first = function (value) {
    console.log('inside the first() function, value = "' + value + '"');
    return 'first';
};
```

```
var second = function (value) {
    console.log('inside the second() function, value = "' + value + '"');
    return 'second';
};

var third = Ext.Function.createSequence(first, second);

var value = third('boom');
console.log('third() returns "' + value + '"');
```

The execution of the code yields the following result in the console:

```
inside the first() function, value = "boom"
inside the second() function, value = "boom"
third() returns "first"
```

createThrottled()

The createThrottled() function is a particularly interesting one: It wraps a function and takes a delay in milliseconds as a parameter; it then filters the execution of the wrapped function, allowing it at least to wait for the specified delay before executing it again.

In the following example, the first call to throttled() executes immediately. However, in the following ones, no matter how many of them are triggered, only one will be executed, and after 4 seconds.

```
var fn = function () {
    console.log('This is being throttled');
};

var throttled = Ext.Function.createThrottled(fn, 4000, this);

// The first call is executed immediately:
throttled();

// No matter how many times we try, this will only be executed
// once, and after 4 seconds:
throttled();
throttled();
throttled();
throttled();
throttled();
throttled();
```

defer()

defer() is used to delay the execution of a function by some milliseconds. The function also takes as parameters the context of execution and, of course, the number of milliseconds before executing the function.

```
Ext.Function.defer(function (arg) {
    console.log('This function has been deferred 1500 ms, arg = "' + arg + '"');
}, 1500, this, [ 'argument1' ]);
```

For more control over delayed execution, check the `Ext.DelayedTask` class, which provides tighter control and more options, including the capability of canceling a scheduled
execution before it happens.

flexSetter()

The `flexSetter()` function is used to provide more flexibility for passing arguments
to functions. When wrapping a function using `flexSetter()`, it can be called using its
original signature or using dictionaries of key-value pairs, allowing to chain assignations
and calls in a more straightforward manner. The method wrapped by `Ext.Func
tion.flexSetter()` must take two arguments.

For example:

```
var setValue = Ext.Function.flexSetter(function(name, value) {
    console.log('name: "' + name + '", value: "' + value + '"');
});

setValue('name1', 'value1');

setValue({
    name2: 'value2',
    name3: 'value3',
    name4: 'value4'
});
```

The preceding code yields the following output in the console; the wrapped function
by `Ext.Function.flexSetter()` is called as many times as required, once for each pair
of name and value parameters:

```
name: "name1", value: "value1"
name: "name2", value: "value2"
name: "name3", value: "value3"
name: "name4", value: "value4"
```

pass()

The `pass()` function is useful to wrap a function and prepopulate the argument list, all
while allowing the wrapper function to pass new arguments to the wrapped function.

```
var originalFunction = function(){
    console.log('inside the original function, arguments:');
    console.dir(Ext.Array.from(arguments));
};

var callback = Ext.Function.pass(originalFunction, ['first', 'second']);
```

```
callback();
callback('third');
```

This code yields the following console messages:

```
inside the original function, arguments:
Array[2]
    0: "first"
    1: "second"

inside the original function, arguments:
Array[3]
    0: "first"
    1: "second"
    2: "third"
```

Ext.JSON

The Ext.JSON object contains an implementation of Douglas Crockford's own JSON parser, including two functions, encode() and decode():

```
var  txt  =  '{"key1":"value1","key2":"2012-11-06T13:24:07","key3":true,"key4":
345.65,"key5":["value2","value3",768]}';
var decoded = Ext.JSON.decode(txt);
console.dir(decoded);

var obj = {
    key1: 'value1',
    key2: new Date(),
    key3: true,
    key4: 345.65,
    key5: [
        'value2',
        'value3',
        768
    ]
};
var encoded = Ext.JSON.encode(obj);
console.log(encoded);
```

Ext.Logger

The Ext.Logger object contains several useful methods that can be used to debug your Sencha Touch applications; you can think of them as extensions and complements to the usual console.log() function that we have been using in this book so far.

deprecate(), error(), log(), and warn()

These four functions provide useful additional information to the developer when verifying the behavior of her code on the console. They include visual hints such as icons and color to provide more information than the usual console.log() statement.

It could not be easier to use them:

```
Ext.Logger.deprecate('this method is deprecated');
Ext.Logger.error('this is an error message');
Ext.Logger.log('this is an generic log message', 0);
Ext.Logger.warn('this is a warning message');
```

The result of the call of these methods appears in Figure 2-3.

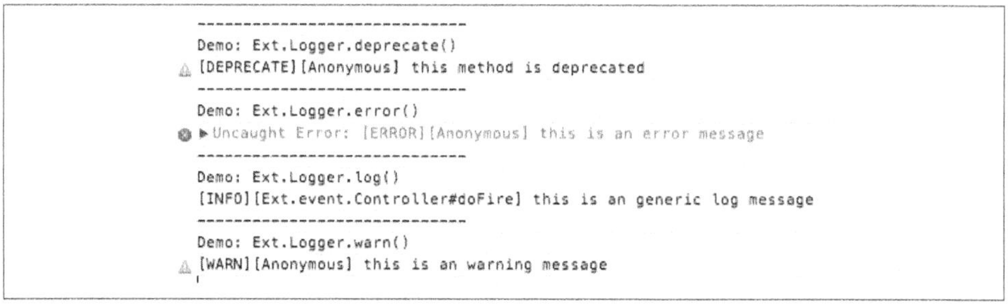

```
------------------------------
Demo: Ext.Logger.deprecate()
⚠ [DEPRECATE][Anonymous] this method is deprecated
------------------------------
Demo: Ext.Logger.error()
⊗ ▶Uncaught Error: [ERROR][Anonymous] this is an error message
------------------------------
Demo: Ext.Logger.log()
[INFO][Ext.event.Controller#doFire] this is an generic log message
------------------------------
Demo: Ext.Logger.warn()
⚠ [WARN][Anonymous] this is an warning message
```

Figure 2-3. Using the Ext.Logger component

Ext.Number

The Ext.Number object contains some functions that provide useful functionality for formatting and verifying numeric input in Sencha Touch applications.

constrain()

This function takes three parameters: a numeric value and minimum and maximum bound values. It then checks whether the first numeric value is located within the minimum and maximum bounds, and if so, it returns it.

```
var constrained = Ext.Number.constrain(234, 0, 6030);
var txt = 'Constrained value: ' + constrained;
console.log(txt);
```

In the preceding code, the value shown will include the constrained value 234, because it is indeed located within the provided range.

from()

The from() function takes two values: a generic value and a default value, which must be numeric; the function then tries to parse a numeric value from the first parameter, and if this is not possible, it will return the default value provided in the second parameter.

```
var num1 = Ext.Number.from('4535', 1111);
var num2 = Ext.Number.from('Some other value', 1111);
var txt1 = 'Retrieved value: ' + num1;
```

```
var txt2 = 'Retrieved value: ' + num2;
console.log(txt1);
console.log(txt2);
```

In the preceding example, the output will be as follows:

```
Retrieved value: 4535
Retrieved value: 1111
```

The first value could be parsed as a numeric input, while the second could not; hence, the default value is returned.

snap()

This function is used to round (or "snap") numbers, providing minimum and maximum bounds at the same time. The first parameter is the number to be rounded; the second parameter is an incremental factor, of which the result of the function will be a multiple; and the final two parameters are minimum and maximum values, used to constrain the final result:

```
var num = Ext.Number.snap(223, 100, 0, 1000);
var txt = 'Snapped value: ' + num;
console.log(txt);
```

The preceding code will show the snapped value "200."

toFixed()

Finally, this function can be used to format a number as a string, using a fixed-point precision that is specified as the second parameter:

```
var num = Ext.Number.toFixed(243.54234534, 2);
var txt = 'Fixed value: ' + num;
console.log(txt);
```

This code will output the value "243.54" on the console.

Ext.Object

Similarly to Ext.Array, the Ext.Object component carries a useful set of functions that extend the native capabilities of JavaScript objects, allowing developers to inspect the state and capabilities of any object.

each()

This function executes a function for every key-value pair in the object.

```
var obj = {
    key1: 'value1',
    key2: 123,
    key3: true
};
```

```
Ext.Object.each(obj, function (key, value) {
    var txt = [key, ': ', value].join('');
    console.log(txt);
}, this);
```

The console output of the preceding code is the following:

```
key1: value1
key2: 123
key3: true
```

fromQueryString() and toQueryString()

These functions perform two reverse operations, allowing the encoding and decoding of complex object structures as simple key-value pairs that could be used as URL parameters.

```
var txt1 = 'key1=value1&key2=123&key3=true';
var obj1 = Ext.Object.fromQueryString(txt1);
console.dir(obj1);

var obj2 = {
    key1: 'value1',
    key2: 123,
    key3: true
};
var txt2 = Ext.Object.toQueryString(obj2);
console.log(txt2);
```

The output of the preceding code is the following:

```
Object
    key1: "value1"
    key2: "123"
    key3: "true"
key1=value1&key2=123&key3=true
```

getKey(), getKeys(), getSize(), getValues()

Predictably enough, these functions provide insight into the internal structure and contents of the object being inspected:

```
var obj = {
    key1: 'value1',
    key2: 123,
    key3: true
};

var key = Ext.Object.getKey(obj, 'value1');
var keys = Ext.Object.getKeys(obj);
var size = Ext.Object.getSize(obj);
var values = Ext.Object.getValues(obj);
```

```
console.dir(key);
console.dir(keys);
console.dir(size);
console.dir(values);
```

The output of the code is quite self-explanatory:

```
key1
Array[3]
    0: "key1"
    1: "key2"
    2: "key3"
    length: 3
3
Array[3]
    0: "value1"
    1: 123
    2: true
    length: 3
```

merge()

The `Ext.Object.merge()` function recursively joins two distinct literal objects; an example will show exactly how this works:

```
var obj1 = {
    key1: 'value1',
    key2: 'value2',
    key3: 345,
    key4: false,
    key5: {
        innerKey1: 'innerValue1'
    }
};
var obj2 = {
    key6: 345,
    key7: 'value1',
    key8: 'value2',
    key9: false,
    key5: {
        innerKey2: 'innerValue1'
    }
};
var merged = Ext.Object.merge(obj1, obj2);
console.dir(merged);
```

The result of this execution is the following:

```
Object
    key1: "value1"
    key2: "value2"
    key3: 345
    key4: false
    key5: Object
```

```
        innerKey1: "innerValue1"
        innerKey2: "innerValue1"
    key6: 345
    key7: "value1"
    key8: "value2"
    key9: false
```

 Ext.Object.merge() is aliased to Ext.merge() for convenience.

toQueryObjects()

This function will encode an object into an array containing name-value pairs that can be used as parameters for sending complex nested structures as part of POST HTTP requests to a server:

```
var obj = {
    day: 5,
    month: 3,
    year: 2002,
    time: {
        hour: 9,
        minute: 20
    }
};
var objs = Ext.Object.toQueryObjects('date', obj, true);
console.dir(objs);
```

The preceding code returns an array object containing the values of the original object in nested keys that can be sent as parameters for a POST HTTP request:

```
Array[5]
    0: Object
        name: "date[day]"
        value: 5
    1: Object
        name: "date[month]"
        value: 3
    2: Object
        name: "date[year]"
        value: 2002
    3: Object
        name: "date[time][hour]"
        value: 9
    4: Object
        name: "date[time][minute]"
        value: 20
    length: 5
```

Ext.String

The `Ext.String` object provides a large array of very useful functions.

capitalize()

This function takes a string as a parameter and returns the same string with its first letter capitalized:

```
var sample = "whatever you shouldn't usually do.";
var txt = Ext.String.capitalize(sample);
console.log(txt);
```

After executing this code, the console shows the text `Whatever you shouldn't usually do.`

ellipsis()

This function cuts the string passed as parameter before the number of characters specified, and adds, if required, an ellipsis at the end; for example, the following code will display the text `whatever you...` in the console.

```
var sample = "whatever you shouldn't usually do.";
var txt = Ext.String.ellipsis(sample, 15);
console.log(txt);
```

escape() and escapeRegex()

These two functions can be used to properly encode characters such as apostrophes, which cannot be properly displayed in some circumstances:

```
var sample = "whatever you shouldn't usually do.";
var txt1 = Ext.String.escape(sample);
var txt2 = Ext.String.escapeRegex(sample);
console.log(txt1);
console.log(txt2);
```

This shows the following text in the console:

```
whatever you shouldn\'t usually do.
whatever you shouldn't usually do\.
```

format()

This function provides a very useful equivalent to the `sprintf()` family of functions available in many other programming languages; it takes a template string, an undefined list of parameters, and it performs the required substitutions:

```
var sample = '<p class="{0}">This is a <strong>{1}</strong></p>';
var txt = Ext.String.format(sample, 'test', 'paragraph');
console.log(txt);
```

The output in the console would be in this case `<p class="test">This is a <strong>paragraph</strong></p>`.

htmlDecode() and htmlEncode()

These two functions perform inverse operations, decoding and encoding characters using their equivalent HTML entities:

```
var sample1 = '&lt;p class=&quot;test&quot;&gt;
This is a &lt;strong&gt;paragraph&lt;/strong&gt;&lt;/p&gt;';
var txt1 = Ext.String.htmlDecode(sample1);
console.log(txt1);

var sample2 = '<p class="test">This is a <strong>paragraph</strong></p>';
var txt2 = Ext.String.htmlEncode(sample2);
console.log(txt2);
```

The console would show the following:

```
<p class="test">This is a <strong>paragraph</strong></p>
&lt;p class=&quot;test&quot;&gt;
This is a &lt;strong&gt;paragraph&lt;/strong&gt;&lt;/p&gt;
```

leftPad(), repeat(), and trim()

These functions are quite self-explanatory:

```
var sample1 = "whatever you shouldn't usually do.";
var txt1 = Ext.String.leftPad(sample, 10, '-');
console.log(txt1);

var txt2 = Ext.String.repeat('=-=-=-=', 50, '/');
console.log(txt2);

var sample3 = "      whatever you shouldn't usually do.        ";
var txt3 = Ext.String.trim(sample3);
console.log(txt3);
```

The output in the console would be:

```
---------------whatever you shouldn't usually do.
=-=-=-=/=-=-=-=/=-=-=-=/=-=-=-=/=-=-=-=/=-=-=-=/=-=-=-=/=-=-=-=/=-=-=-=
whatever you shouldn't usually do.
```

toggle()

This function provides a very simple way to display mutually exclusive strings depending on a simple condition: whenever one value is passed as parameter, the other is returned:

```
var txt = 'No';
txt = Ext.String.toggle(txt, 'Yes', 'No');
console.log(txt);
```

In the preceding code, the string Yes would be returned by the function.

urlAppend()

This function takes care of serializing and appending encoded parameters to a URL:

```
var sample = 'http://test.com/whatever';
var params = {
    key1: 'value1',
    key2: true,
    key3: 34536.65
};
var paramsTxt = Ext.Object.toQueryString(params);
var txt = Ext.String.urlAppend(sample, paramsTxt);
console.log(txt);
```

The preceding code would return the following: http://test.com/whatever?
key1=value1&key2=true&key3=34536.65.

Ext.Version

The Ext.Version object contains functions that manipulate version information. With them you can verify, compare, and extract information out of version strings, such as "1.0," "2.5.6," or even "6.2.5alpha"; the following code summarizes the most important capabilities offered by these functions:

```
var currentVersion = Ext.version;
var version = Ext.create('Ext.Version', currentVersion);

var results = {};
results.equals = version.equals('1.0');
results.build = version.getBuild();
results.major = version.getMajor();
results.minor = version.getMinor();
results.patch = version.getPatch();
results.release = version.getRelease();
results.shortVersion = version.getShortVersion();
results.greaterThan1 = version.isGreaterThan('1.0');
results.greaterThanOrEqual1 = version.isGreaterThanOrEqual('1.0');
results.lessThan1 = version.isLessThan('1.0');
results.lessThanOrEqual1 = version.isLessThanOrEqual('1.0');
results.match = version.match('5.0');
results.array = version.toArray();

Ext.Object.each(results, function (key, value) {
    console.log(key + '> "' + value + '"');
}, this);
```

The preceding code would display the following in the console:

```
equals> "false"
build> "0"
```

```
major> "2"
minor> "1"
patch> "0"
release> ""
shortVersion> "210"
greaterThan1> "true"
greaterThanOrEqual1> "true"
lessThan1> "false"
lessThanOrEqual1> "false"
match> "false"
array> "2,1,0,0,"
```

Ext.mixin.Observable

The Ext.mixin.Observable mixin is the component that enables Sencha Touch objects to publish, fire, and listen to events; in the following example, the Animal class uses the mixin so that instances of it can listen to individual eating and beingEaten events, which are fired by the eat() method:

```
// Defining the animal class
Ext.define('Animal', {
    mixins: ['Ext.mixin.Observable'],

    config: {
        name: '(some animal name here)',
        kind: '(animal kind here)'
    },

    constructor: function(config) {
        this.initConfig(config);
    },

    eat: function (animal) {
        // Here is where the magic happens
        this.fireEvent('eating', animal);
        animal.fireEvent('beingEaten', this);
    }
});

// Creating two instances of the Animal class
var lion = Ext.create('Animal', {
    name: 'Simba',
    kind: 'Lion',
    listeners: {
        eating: function (prey) {
            var template = '{0} the {1} is eating {2} the {3}!';
            var name = this.getName();
            var kind = this.getKind();
            var preyName = prey.getName();
            var preyKind = prey.getKind();
            var txt = Ext.String.format(template, name, kind, preyName,
```

```
            preyKind);
            console.log(txt);
        }
    }
});

var zebra = Ext.create('Animal', {
    name: 'Pumbaa',
    kind: 'Warthog',
    listeners: {
        beingEaten: function (predator) {
            var template = '{0} the {1} is being eaten by {2} the {3}!';
            var name = this.getName();
            var kind = this.getKind();
            var predName = predator.getName();
            var predKind = predator.getKind();
            var txt = Ext.String.format(template, name, kind, predName,
            predKind);
            console.log(txt);
        }
    }
});

// And now nature follows its path
lion.eat(zebra);
```

Ext.util.DelayedTask

The `Ext.util.DelayedTask` provides a simple API around the standard `setTime
out()` and `clearTimeout()` functions of the standard JavaScript library. DelayedTask
instances can be delayed and canceled using a very simple API:

```
var task = Ext.create('Ext.util.DelayedTask', function() {
    console.log('This message took 1.5 seconds to appear');
});

task.delay(1500);
```

Predictably enough, the `cancel()` method can be called on tasks to prevent their execution.

What is the difference with `Ext.defer()`?

`Ext.util.DelayedTask` objects wrap a function to be called at some
point in the future. These objects also expose the `cancel()` method,
giving more control to the developer, as the task not only can be passed
as parameter to other parts of the application, but it can also be canceled
if needed. On the other hand, the `Ext.Function.defer()` provides a
non-cancelable, one-shot execution of a function.

Ext.util.HashMap

The Ext.util.HashMap is a container class that can be used in lieu of standard JavaScript literal dictionaries; it provides a very simple API and, most importantly, it exposes useful events that allow applications to be notified when items are added or removed from these containers.

add(), clear(), remove(), removeByKey(), replace()

These methods are used to manipulate the items inside an Ext.util.HashMap instance. They all trigger the execution of the corresponding events:

- add
- clear
- remove
- replace

The following code shows an example of use:

```
var map = Ext.create('Ext.util.HashMap');
map.on('add', function (map, key, value, eOpts) {
    console.log('EVENT; item added; key: "' + key + '",
    value: "' + value + '"');
});
map.on('clear', function (map, eOpts) {
    console.log('EVENT; map cleared');
});
map.on('remove', function (map, key, value, eOpts) {
    console.log('EVENT; item removed; key: "' + key + '",
    value: "' + value + '"');
});
map.on('replace', function (map, key, value, old, eOpts) {
    console.log('EVENT; item replaced; key: "' + key + '", old value: "' +
    old  +'", new value: "' + value + '"');
});

map.add('key1', 'value1');
map.add('key2', 1234);
map.add('key3', true);
map.clear();

map.add('key1', 'value1');
map.add('key2', 1234);
map.add('key3', true);
map.remove(true);
map.removeByKey('key2');
map.replace('key2', 'new value');
```

contains(), containsKey()

These two functions are used to test for the existence of values (or keys) in a particular instance.

```
var map = Ext.create('Ext.util.HashMap');
map.add('key1', 'value1');
map.add('key2', 1234);
map.add('key3', true);

console.log('Map contains "value1" : ' + map.contains('value1'));
console.log('Map contains "key2" : ' + map.containsKey('key2'));
```

each()

The each( ) method takes a function as parameter; this function is called for each key-value pair in the hash map following the iterator pattern.

```
var map = Ext.create('Ext.util.HashMap');
map.add('key1', 'value1');
map.add('key2', 1234);
map.add('key3', true);

map.each(function (key, value) {
    var txt = key + '> ' + value;
    console.log(txt);
});
```

get(), getCount(), getKeys(), getValues()

These functions are used to inspect the current state of the instance.

```
var map = Ext.create('Ext.util.HashMap');
map.add('key1', 'value1');
map.add('key2', 1234);
map.add('key3', true);

console.log('Map has ' + map.getCount() + ' values');

var obj = map.get('key1');
console.log('object with key "key1" = "' + obj + '"');

var keys = map.getKeys();
console.dir(keys);

var values = map.getValues();
console.dir(values);
```

Ext.util.Inflector

The Ext.util.Inflector class provides some utility functions that are used to manage the pluralization and singularization of words in English.

---

isTransnumeral()

In English, a transnumeral word is a word that does not change when used in plural or singular forms.

```
var words = ['fish', 'people', 'gents', 'women', 'happiness', 'sheep', 'code'];
Ext.iterate(words, function (item) {
    var txt = [item, ' is transnumeral: ',
    Ext.util.Inflector.isTransnumeral(item)].join('');
    console.log(txt);
}, this);
```

This yields the following console output:

```
fish is transnumeral: true
people is transnumeral: false
gents is transnumeral: false
women is transnumeral: false
happiness is transnumeral: false
sheep is transnumeral: true
code is transnumeral: false
```

ordinalize()

This function takes a number as a parameter and returns the proper ordinal string:

```
var words = [1, 2, 3, 4, 5, 345, 456, 822, 21, 80];
Ext.iterate(words, function (item) {
    var txt = Ext.util.Inflector.ordinalize(item);
    console.log(txt);
}, this);
```

The result is the following:

```
1st
2nd
3rd
4th
5th
345th
456th
822nd
21st
80th
```

pluralize(), singularize()

These functions take a word in either plural and singular form and return the opposite version.

```
var singular = ['person', 'country', 'mouse', 'thing', 'boom'];
Ext.iterate(singular, function (item) {
    var txt = ['One', item, 'many',
    Ext.util.Inflector.pluralize(item)].join(' ');
```

```
        console.log(txt);
}, this);

var plural = ['people', 'countries', 'mice', 'things', 'booms'];
Ext.iterate(plural, function (item) {
    var txt = ['Many', item, 'one',
    Ext.util.Inflector.singularize(item)].join(' ');
    console.log(txt);
}, this);
```

This is the result:

```
One person many people
One country many countries
One mouse many mice
One thing many things
One boom many booms
Many people one person
Many countries one country
Many mice one mouse
Many things one thing
Many booms one boom
```

Conclusion

This chapter provided an introduction to the Sencha Touch class system, used to define classes and to create new instances out of those classes. We have also taken a look at the different class families available in the framework, and we have studied more about the low-level code utilities integrated into Sencha Touch, which remove the need for external libraries.

## CHAPTER 3

Views

Views are the most visible element of any application; using view components, developers can assemble and create the UIs of their applications, the same ones their users will learn to love (or hate) as they use their software—although the team at Sencha seems to have done all it can to make sure users love the applications built with this framework!

Sencha Touch has an unprecedented number of high-level components, ready to be used in your applications; these components fit together quite nicely and have a vast array of events that can be used to provide interactivity. This chapter will delve into all of these aspects in detail and will provide an overview of the most important UI classes available in the framework.

Components, Containers, and Panels

All the visual components of Sencha Touch inherit from a base class called `Ext.Compo` `nent`. Components can draw themselves on the screen; they can be shown and hidden, enabled and disabled at any time; they can be resized, moved, and animated; and finally they can also trigger events, allowing developers to react to user input or to changing conditions.

However, if you look at the class inheritance of most Sencha Touch view components, you are going to see that many inherit also from `Ext.Container`. It turns out that containers are a special kind of component that can also contain (hence the name) other child components inside. This means that containers can add and remove child components, as well as arranging them in layouts.

Finally, some other containers, such as message boxes, inherit from `Ext.Panel`, itself a subclass of `Ext.Container`. Panels can be shown as overlays on top of other components, including animations and transitions.

Events

One of the most useful things about components is that they can trigger events. Events in Sencha Touch view components can be added in two separate locations:

- On the view definition itself, using the `listeners` configuration entry
- On a separate controller class

You can mix and match both approaches; this means that when an event is fired, all the functions configured as event handlers for that particular event will fire (in no particular order, though).

Controllers will be described in detail in Chapter 6.

The following code shows a very simple event handler for a button:

```
{
    xtype: 'button',
    text: 'Action button',
    listeners: {
        tap: function (button, e, eOpts) {
            console.log('Button was tapped');
        }
    }
}
```

In the preceding example, we are using the simplest of all Sencha Touch components: the button, represented by the class `Ext.Button` or its xtype `button`. Inside this button definition, we attach a function to the `tap` event, which is fired whenever the button is touched.

Event handler parameters
Event handler functions like the preceding take myriad parameters; it is a very good programming practice to always check the documentation for the proper function signature of each event handler and to add all of those parameters. Even if they are not useful at first sight, you might need to use them later.

Typical events in Sencha Touch include the following:

- The `initialize`, `hide`, and `show` events in the `Ext.Component` class

- The add and remove events in the Ext.Container class, which are triggered every time subviews are added or removed from a parent component
- The scrollstart, scroll, and scrollend events in the Ext.scroll.Scroller class, which is used internally by components that are scrollable
- The tap event in the Ext.Button class (as shown in the previous example)
- The itemtap, itemsingletap, itemdoubletap, and disclose events in the Ext.data.List class
- The maprender event in the Ext.Map
- The toggle event in the Ext.SegmentedButton class
- The play, pause, stop, and ended events in the Ext.Video and Ext.Audio classes
- The back, pop, and push events in the Ext.navigation.View class
- The focus and blur events in the Ext.field.Text class (to be studied in detail in Chapter 5)

As you can see, the number of events is huge; application developers can be notified at any moment of any activity in any component, just by attaching functions wherever required. Remember to check the documentation for the proper signatures of the functions!

Layouts

As we have seen, containers are a type of component that can hold other components as children. This is done through the use of the items property, which takes an array of component instances.

JavaScript arrays only specify order, but containers need more information than just order to render themselves in the screen; they need to know where to position each child component before being drawn.

To give containers a hint about the relative positions of each child component on the screen, developers specify a layout configuration property, which describes an instance of any of the subclasses of Ext.layout.Default. There are several layouts available:

- fit, which is the simplest of all the available layouts, and which makes the child component completely fit the available space of its parent
- hbox, which stacks child views horizontally
- vbox, used to stack child components vertically
- card, used to stack several components on the same structure but display only one at a time (particularly useful in smartphone screens)

Additionally, every layout is able to dock components, which is used to force some components to be placed at the edges (top, right, bottom, or left), resizing the other components if required.

The first layout is fit, which is by far the easiest to understand; it just tells its receiver to occupy the whole space made available by its parent, as shown in the following example:

```
Ext.define('Chapter3Layouts.view.FitDemo', {
    extend: 'Ext.Container',
    xtype: 'fitdemo',
    config: {
        layout: {
            type: 'fit'
        },
        items: [{
            xtype: 'component', margin: 10,
            html: 'This component is set to fit',
            style: 'background-color: lightgray'
        }]
    }
});
```

The result of the code is shown in Figure 3-1.

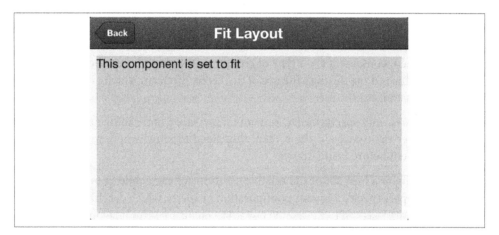

Figure 3-1. Fit layout

The second layout is hbox, which is very similar to vbox, with only a major difference: the orientation of the resulting layout. In both cases, though, the child views must have a flex configuration parameter, which works as follows:

1. The layout sums all the values of the flex parameter in the child views.

2. The available space for the child views is divided evenly using the formula "flex / (sum of flex values)."

In the following example, the flex values are 1 and 3, which means that the sum is 4; in that case, the first view receives one-fourth of the available space, while the second view receives three-fourths of it.

```
Ext.define('Chapter3Layouts.view.HBoxDemo', {
    extend: 'Ext.Container',
    xtype: 'hboxdemo',
    config: {
        defaults: {
            margin: 10
        },
        layout: {
            type: 'hbox'
        },
        items: [{
            xtype: 'component', flex: 1,
            html: 'Flex: 1', style: 'background-color: pink'
        }, {
            xtype: 'component', flex: 3,
            html: 'Flex: 3', style: 'background-color: lightgray'
        }]
    }
});
```

The code for the vbox layout demo is strictly the same, apart from the layout: 'vbox' parameter. The resulting UIs are shown in Figure 3-2 and Figure 3-3.

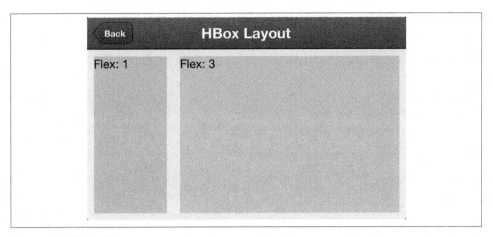

Figure 3-2. HBox layout

The card layout is probably the most important of all, as it provides a way to easily switch among views in devices with little screen real estate, such as smartphones.

In a card layout, the only view that is visible by default is the first one in the items array, while the others are hidden "beneath" the first one. To switch to any other view, just call the setActiveItem() function (which is added automatically to any container that uses the card layout, but is not available otherwise) and the view will switch accordingly, with an animation if required.

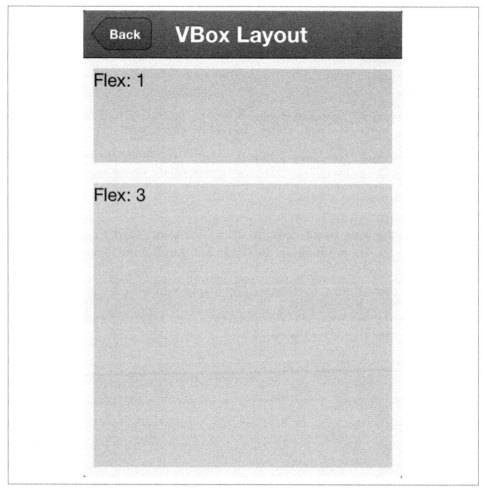

Figure 3-3. VBox layout

The following source code yields the result shown in Figure 3-4.

```
Ext.define('Chapter3Layouts.view.CardDemo', {
    extend: 'Ext.Container',
    xtype: 'carddemo',
    config: {
        defaults: {
            margin: 10
        },
        layout: {
            type: 'card'
        },
        items: [{
            xtype: 'segmentedbutton',
            docked: 'top',
            items: [{
                text: 'First', pressed: true
            }, {
                text: 'Second'
            }, {
                text: 'Third'
            }],
            listeners: {
                toggle: function (segmentedbutton, button, isPressed, eOpts) {
                    if (isPressed) {
                        var container = segmentedbutton.getParent();
                        var txt = button.getText()
                        var selectedComponent = container.getComponent
                        (button.getText());
                        container.setActiveItem(selectedComponent); // ❶
                    }
                }
            }
        }, {
            xtype: 'component', itemId: 'First',
            html: 'First component', style: 'background-color: pink'
        }, {
            xtype: 'component', itemId: 'Second',
            html: 'Second component', style: 'background-color: lightgray'
        }, {
            xtype: 'component', itemId: 'Third',
            html: 'Third component', style: 'background-color: cyan'
        }]
    }
});
```

❶   The call to the setActiveItem() triggers the change from one view to the other.

The card layout is used extensively throughout Sencha Touch; for example, the
Ext.Viewport singleton instance uses it by default, as well as many complex containers
such as the Ext.tab.Panel and the Ext.carousel.Carousel classes.

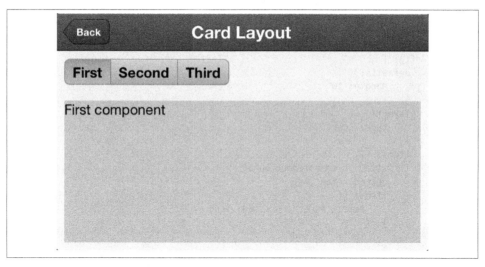

Figure 3-4. Card layout

Finally, you can override some layout properties and force the location of some subviews using the docked property, which takes four self-explanatory values: top, bottom, right, and left. Figure 3-5 shows the result of having a fit layout with a view in the center, surrounded by four other views docked at the edges of the screen.

```
Ext.define('Chapter3Layouts.view.DockingDemo', {
    extend: 'Ext.Container',
    xtype: 'dockingdemo',
    config: {
        defaults: {
            margin: 5
        },
        layout: {
            type: 'fit'
        },
        items: [{
            xtype: 'component', docked: 'top', html: 'Docking: "top"',
            style: 'background-color: pink'
        }, {
            xtype: 'component', docked: 'left', html: '"left"',
            style: 'background-color: lightblue'
        }, {
            xtype: 'component', docked: 'right', html: '"right"',
            style: 'background-color: lightgreen'
        }, {
            xtype: 'component', docked: 'bottom', html: 'Docking: "bottom"',
            style: 'background-color: cyan'
        }, {
            xtype: 'component', html: 'Centered',
            style: 'background-color: lightgray'
```

```
        }]
    }
});
```

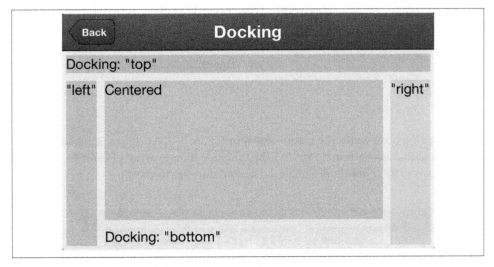

Figure 3-5. Docking views

Templates

The Sencha Touch view subsystem also uses templating to generate dynamic HTML code, in a similar way as mustache (*http://mustache.github.com/*), jQuery templates (*http://api.jquery.com/category/plugins/templates/*), or pure (*http://beebole.com/pure/*) do.

The Sencha Touch template system is based in the Ext.XTemplate class and is also baked in the Ext.Component class through the tpl configuration parameter.

In the example that follows, we populate a container with the tpl parameter, instead of using the simpler html configuration. This allows developers to consume complex sets of data and to display them in intricate ways:

```
Ext.define('Chapter3Layouts.view.TemplatesDemo', {
    extend: 'Ext.Container',
    xtype: 'templatesdemo',
    config: {
        scrollable: true,
        data: {
            countries: [{
                country: 'Argentina', flagColors: ['light blue', 'white']
            }, {
                country: 'Switzerland', flagColors: ['red', 'white']
            }, {
```

```
                        country: 'France', flagColors: ['blue', 'white', 'red']
                    }]
                },
                tpl: Ext.create('Ext.XTemplate', '<tpl for="countries">',
                            '<div>{#}. {country}: {flagColors:this.join}</div>',
                            '</tpl>',
                            {
                                join: function (value) {
                                    return value.join(', ');
                                }
                            })
            }
        });
```

The preceding code yields the result shown in Figure 3-6. As shown, templates can be extended with custom functions, and they include a large array of built-in functions that deal with string manipulation and date and number formatting.

Figure 3-6. Using templates

Component Library Catalog

Sencha Touch, like many other large, "enterprisey" programming frameworks, offers an incredible library of components ready to be used in applications. This section will go through most of them, providing examples of use, screenshots, and usage guidelines for them.

 This section will not cover data-bound views, which are covered in Chapter 4, or form fields, which are covered in extensive detail in Chapter 5. However, those are components and, in some cases, also containers.

The diagram in Figure 3-7 shows a simplified overview of the hierarchy of view classes available in Sencha Touch 2.1 (for the sake of readability, not all view classes are represented in the diagram). This chapter considers three major families of components:

- Basic components, inheriting from `Ext.Component`
- Containers, inheriting from `Ext.Container`
- Panels, inheriting from `Ext.Panel`

This chapter also adds yet another group to these families: the "Multimedia" components, allowing developers to include complex visualizations such as audio, video, or graphs. These components are usually just subclasses of `Ext.Component`, but they deserve a place of their own, as they encapsulate exceptionally useful functionality behind surprisingly simple interfaces.

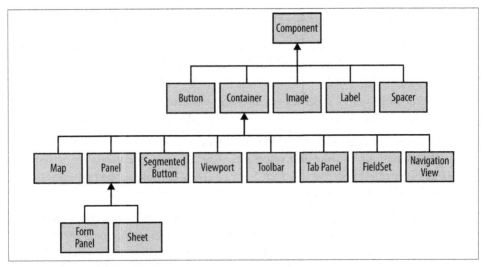

Figure 3-7. View classes hierarchy diagram (simplified)

Let's review each of these class families in detail.

Components

The first family of visual elements available in the Sencha Touch framework includes direct subclasses of Ext.Component. In this group we find common and simple elements such as buttons and labels.

All components in Sencha Touch (which basically means anything you can see on the screen of your Sencha Touch application) can be configured using these properties:

- The `centered` property is a Boolean value that specifies whether the current instance must be centered inside its parent container.

- The `contentEl` property allows developers to populate a Sencha Touch component with any HTML element available in the page; the property can hold an `Ext.Element` object, a DOM reference, or a string with an element ID.

- The `disabled` property is a Boolean that specifies whether the current component is active or not, to receive user input and to react to events. Please pay attention to the fact that there is no `enabled` property!

- The `docked` property specifies the location where to anchor a particular component on a complex layout; the valid values for this parameter are `top`, `bottom`, `left`, and `right`.

- The `flex` property is used by the `hbox` and `vbox` layouts to specify the proportion of screen real estate to be reserved to a particular component. Please refer to the "Layouts" section later in this chapter for more information about them.

- The `fullscreen` property is used when a component is directly added to the `Ext.Viewport` singleton instance of the application; this Boolean specifies whether the component in question has to stretch itself to occupy the whole space available.

- The `hidden` property specifies whether the current component is visible or not. Please pay attention to the fact that there is no `visible` property available!

- The `hideAnimation` and `showAnimation` properties provide very simple ways to apply animations to your user interfaces. You can specify either a string with the name of an animation (such as `fadeIn` or `pop`) or a complex object representing an instance of the `Ext.Anim` class.

- The `itemId` property should always be preferred instead of the more common `id` property; this is because the `itemId` property requires uniqueness of value only among child components of a container, while the `id` property requires all values to be different throughout the whole application, which can be difficult to use. The values of the `itemId` property are usually used with the `Ext.Container.getCompo nent()` instance function, which is used to retrieve pointers of child components inside a container.

- `maxHeight`, `maxWidth`, `minHeight`, and `minWidth` are used to constrain the size of the current instance, making sure that the automatic layout process of the application respects some basic boundaries.

- The style property allows developers to inject any kind of CSS string that they wish directly into the application. Although this is convenient, it would be wiser to use the cls property instead, which specifies additional CSS classes, defined in an external CSS file.

- Finally, the styleHtmlContent Boolean property (whose value is false by default) specifies whether the value of the html property can be styled or not (for example, when using HTML text that contains <strong>, <em>, or <a> tags, which carry their own styling semantics).

Button

Buttons are the most common user interface element in any visual widget toolkit. As expected, creating buttons in Sencha Touch could not be simpler, using the Ext.Button class (or the button xtype):

```
{
    xtype: 'button',
    text: 'Reply',
    badgeText: '42',
    ui: 'normal',
    iconCls: 'reply',
    iconMask: true,
    iconAlign: 'top',
    margin: '5 5 5 30',
    listeners: {
        tap: function (button, e, eOpts) {
            console.log('button tap');
        }
    }
}
```

The result of the preceding code can be seen in Figure 3-8.

Figure 3-8. Button example

Button instances can be configured in several different ways:

- The `text` property specifies the label displayed by the button.

- The `badgeText` property provides a value to be shown on a red badge on top of the button, to notify the user about some particular situation.

- The `ui` property can take several values: *action, back, confirm, decline, forward, normal, plain,* and *round.* Applying any of these values will change the shape and color of the button, providing context and hints about the functionality of the button to the user. See Figure 3-9 for examples of setting different values to the `ui` property.

- Buttons can have icons applied to them. Using the `iconCls` property together with the `iconMask: true` property, you can use a large array of default icons provided by Sencha Touch: *action, add, arrow_down, arrow_left, arrow_right, arrow_up, bookmarks, compose, delete, download, favorites, home, info, locate, maps, more, organize, refresh,* and *reply.* See Figure 3-10 for some examples.

- The `iconAlign` property can be used to change the relative position of the icon to the text; it accepts the values *top, right, bottom, left,* and *center.* You can see some of these positions in Figure 3-10.

- Finally, the `listeners` property allows developers to attach event handlers to individual buttons, although this can also be done using controllers.

 Remember to set `iconMask: true` whenever using the default icons provided by Sencha Touch; otherwise these will not be visible in the button.

Figure 3-9. Buttons with different UI properties

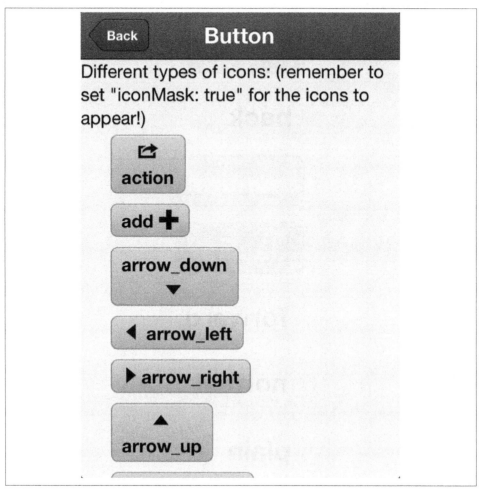

Figure 3-10. Buttons with different icons

Label

The Ext.Label class (xtype label) is probably the simplest of all the components available in Sencha Touch; it just provides a placeholder to display any HTML text inside of your application. Creating one of these, as usual, involves a very simple operation:

```
{
    xtype: 'label',
    html: 'This is a label; it can display any kind of HTML or plain text.'
}
```

Containers

As previously explained, containers are a special kind of component that can contain other components. We are going to learn about the most important containers available:

- Carousel
- Navigation view
- Segmented button
- Tab panel
- Title bar
- Toolbar

Containers allow developers to organize large applications into the small screens available in smartphones and tablets. They provide visual cues for users to find their way, including animation and indicators.

In addition to the configuration options provided by the Ext.Component class, containers can be customized using several more properties:

- The most important property of containers is, without doubt, the items property, which defines the child elements to be embedded inside it.

- The defaultType property specifies the xtype of the child elements of a particular container; for example, toolbars expect their children to be buttons, while tab panels expect them to be just components, and so on. You can define your own expected value for this property, and automatically all components defined inside the items property will be instances of that type (unless you specify a custom xtype, of course).

- The defaults property specifies common properties for all the child components defined inside the current container.

- The layout property specifies the arrangement for the child elements of a container. Since the items property is just a linear array, Sencha Touch needs to have more information on how to distribute the elements of this array. The layout property provides that information.

- Finally, the scrollable property specifies whether the component can scroll to reveal child components not visible otherwise.

Let's now study the most important containers available in Sencha Touch.

Carousel

The Ext.carousel.Carousel class (xtype carousel) simply stacks child views horizontally or vertically and allows the user to swipe from one to the other. The component also provides a visual indicator at the bottom of the screen (or at the right side when using the vertical direction setting), giving the user an indication of the total number of pages available, as well as a hint about the current one:

```
{
    xtype: 'carousel',
    fullscreen: true,
    direction: 'vertical',
    items: [{
        html: 'Red',
        style: 'background-color: red'
    }, {
        html: 'Yellow',
        style: 'background-color: yellow'
    }, {
        html: 'Green',
        style: 'background-color: green'
    }]
}
```

The result of the code is a screen that looks like Figure 3-11, as the user scrolls from the second to the third embedded component.

Navigation view

The Ext.navigation.View class provides a stack-based navigation component that is heavily inspired by the UINavigationController class of iOS. A navigation view allows users to drill down in data from general to more specific categories, all while being able to return to the previous screen using a Back button, conveniently located on the upper-left side of the screen.

The navigation view itself is a container that does not show lots of UI chrome to the users besides the navigation bar and the Back button itself. However, it offers a very interesting interface to application developers, who can programmatically use the push() and pop() functions to add and remove views, triggering an animation and the display of the next screen in the sequence.

 You can see examples of the Ext.navigation.View class in action when browsing the code examples in a smartphone device.

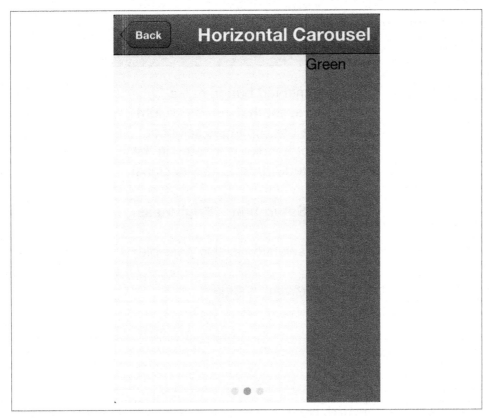

Figure 3-11. Carousel in action

Segmented button

Segmented buttons provide a finger-sized alternative to radio buttons. They are (as many other components in Sencha Touch) heavily inspired by their iOS cousin, the `UISegmentedControl` class.

Creating a segmented button, as usual, is a straightforward task:

```
{
    xtype: 'segmentedbutton',
    items: [{
        text: 'Hue'
    }, {
        text: 'Saturation'
    }, {
        text: 'Brightness'
    }]
}
```

The result is shown in Figure 3-12.

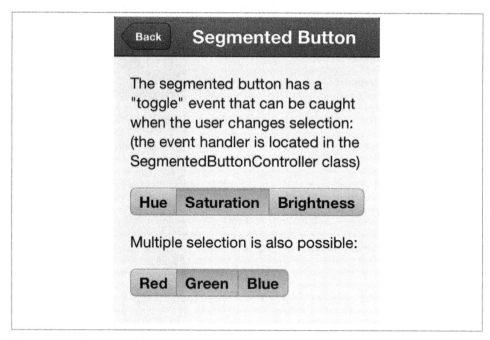

Figure 3-12. Segmented buttons

Tab panel

If navigation views are stack-based containers, helping users to navigate sequentially between components, then you can think of tab panels as array-based containers, enabling random navigation among components.

As usual, configuring a tab panel involves filling the items array with some components:

```
{
    xtype: 'tabpanel',
    layout: {
        // Possible values: cover, cube, fade, flip, pop, reveal, scroll, slide
        // You can also specify "false" (Boolean value) to disable all
        // animations
        animation: 'flip'
    },
    tabBarPosition: 'bottom',
    items: [{
        title: 'Profile',
        iconCls: 'user', iconMask: true,
        style: 'background-color: #e17467; color: white',
        html: 'Your profile screen here'
    }, {
        title: 'Favorites',
        iconCls: 'favorites', iconMask: true,
```

```
        style: 'background-color: #f6eb69',
        html: 'Your favorites here'
    }, {
        title: 'Search',
        iconCls: 'search', iconMask: true,
        style: 'background-color: #74e796',
        html: 'Search engine here'
    }, {
        title: 'Action',
        iconCls: 'action', iconMask: true,
        style: 'background-color: #688ee2',
        html: 'Do something here'
    }, {
        title: 'More',
        iconCls: 'more', iconMask: true,
        style: 'background-color: lightgray',
        html: 'There is lots you can do here'
    }]
}
```

The result of the preceding configuration can be seen in Figure 3-13.

Figure 3-13. Tab panel

Using the `tabBarPosition: 'top'` value will send the tab bar to the top, which is a common choice for Android applications. In that case, the result will be similar to the one shown in Figure 3-14, and given the increased width of the individual buttons in the tab bar, developers should include an additional configuration option to increase the usability of the component:

```
{
    xtype: 'tabpanel',
    tabBarPosition: 'top',
    tabBar: {
        scrollable: true
    },
    // ...
}
```

Thanks to the `activeitemchange` event (defined in the `Ext.Container` class) developers can be notified of the fact that the user has selected a different screen using the tab bar.

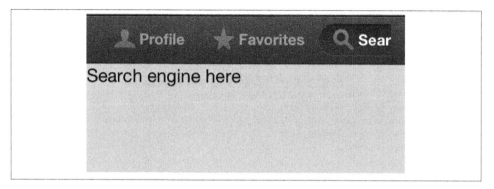

Figure 3-14. Tab panel with tab bar on top

Title bars and toolbars

Title bars (represented by the `Ext.TitleBar` class or the `titlebar` xtype) and toolbars (`Ext.Toolbar`, or simply `toolbar`) are very similar components; the main difference between them is that the `title` configuration in the title bar is always centered, while the toolbar does not make this assumption. In both cases, though, the `docked` configuration (usually `top` or `bottom`) is used to attach the component to a specific location of its parent container.

The following source code shows how to create a very simple toolbar with some buttons in it:

```
{
    xtype: 'toolbar', docked: 'bottom',
    items: [{
        iconCls: 'favorites', iconMask: true
```

```
    }, {
        xtype: 'spacer'
    }, {
        iconCls: 'search', iconMask: true
    }]
}
```

A spacer object (officially, a component of type Ext.Spacer) inserts a flexible space between buttons, allowing a group of buttons to be "pushed" to the right side of the screen automatically. This object is familiar to iOS developers, who can use a UIBar ButtonItem instance, with the SystemItem parameter set to UIBarButtonSystemItem FlexibleSpace in pretty much the same way.

To create a title bar, it is as simple as usual; in this case, the title will be automatically centered.

```
{
    xtype: 'titlebar', docked: 'top', title: 'Top',
    items: [{
        iconCls: 'action', iconMask: true, align: 'left', text: 'Action'
    }, {
        iconCls: 'user', iconMask: true, align: 'right', text: 'Profile'
    }]
}
```

The result of the preceding code snippets can be seen in Figure 3-15.

Viewport

The Ext.Viewport is a singleton instance, created automatically for you when an MVC Sencha Touch application is launched through the Ext.application() function (or the Ext.setup() function for non-MVC apps). The Viewport is set to fullscreen: true by default and is meant to be populated with the views that make up the application. It is also configured with a "card" layout ready to be used out of the box.

 In a sense, the Viewport in Sencha Touch can be thought of as the single UIWindow instance used in iOS applications or the root Activity in Android applications—the place where the UI is built from scratch and populated.

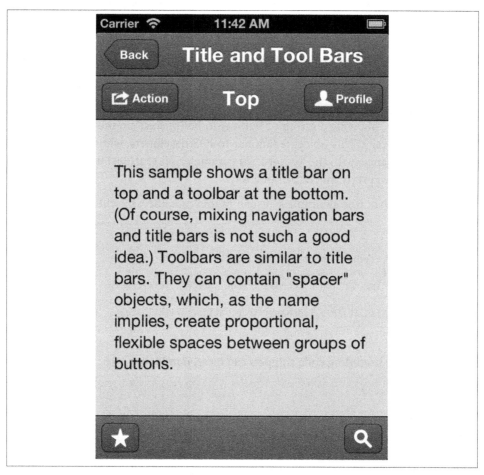

Figure 3-15. Title bar and toolbar

The Ext.Viewport singleton is most often used in the launch() function, either in the main app.js file or in the individual profiles for different device types, like in the following example:

```
Ext.define('Chapter3Views.profile.Tablet', {
    extend: 'Ext.app.Profile',
    config: {
        name: 'Tablet',
        models: [],
        views: ['AkoLib.view.SplitView'],
        controllers: ['TabletController']
    },
    isActive: function () {
        return Ext.os.is.Tablet || Ext.os.is.Desktop;
    },
```

```
    launch: function () {
        Ext.Viewport.add({
            xtype: 'akosplitview',
            screenTitle: 'View Catalog',
            menuButtonTitle: 'Demos',
            masterView: {
                xtype:
                'indexview'
            },
            detailView: {
                xtype: 'panel',
                html: 'Choose a demo from the menu'
            }
        });
    }
});
```

Panels

Panels (instances of the Ext.Panel class, with the xtype panel) are a special kind of container that can be used as overlay views, floating on top of other components. The most important API they offer developers is the showBy() function, which takes any other component as a parameter and makes the panel appear "pointing" to it. Figure 3-16 shows an example of a panel appearing near a button, as defined in the following code:

```
{
    xtype: 'button',
    text: 'Touch to open panel',
    itemId: 'openPanelButton',
    listeners: {
        tap: function (button, e, eOpts) {
            if (!button.panel) {
                button.panel = Ext.widget('panel', {
                    html: 'This is a panel',
                    padding: 20,
                    width: 280,
                    modal: true,
                    hideOnMaskTap: true, // ❶
                    hidden: true,
                    hideAnimation: 'fadeOut',
                    showAnimation: 'fadeIn'
                });
            }
            button.panel.showBy(button);
        }
    }
}
```

❶   This is a very useful configuration to set on panels, so that users can dismiss the panel just by hitting anywhere around it.

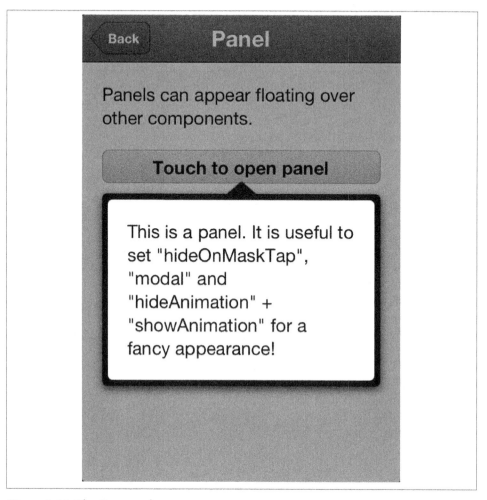

Figure 3-16. Floating panel

Many components in Sencha Touch extend panels to display fancy overlays in applications:

- Action sheets
- Message boxes
- Pickers
- Sheets

In the following sections, we are going to see each one of these subclasses.

Action sheet

Action sheets (represented by the xtype `actionsheet` or its equivalent, the `Ext.Action Sheet` class) are also inspired by its iOS counterpart. They are commonly used to display a modal interface allowing the user to choose from a restricted set of buttons, typically to perform some operation on the current screen.

The following code shows how to configure and use an action sheet:

```
{
    xtype: 'button',
    text: 'Touch to open action sheet',
    itemId: 'openButton',
    listeners: {
        tap: function (button, e, eOpts) {
            if (!button.sheet) {
                button.sheet = Ext.widget('actionsheet', {
                    items: [{
                        text: 'Delete',
                        listeners: {
                            tap: function (btn, e, eOpts) {
                                button.sheet.hide();
                            }
                        }
                    }, {
                        text: 'Approve',
                        ui: 'confirm',
                        listeners: {
                            tap: function (btn, e, eOpts) {
                                button.sheet.hide();
                            }
                        }
                    }, {
                        text: 'Cancel',
                        ui: 'decline',
                        listeners: {
                            tap: function (btn, e, eOpts) {
                                button.sheet.hide();
                            }
                        }
                    }]
                });
                Ext.Viewport.add(button.sheet); // ❶
            }
            button.sheet.show(); // ❷
        }
    }
}
```

❶   You must add the sheet to the current Viewport before using it!

❷   To display the sheet, just call its `show()` function.

The result of the preceding code is shown in Figure 3-17.

Figure 3-17. Action sheet in action

Message box

Message boxes are triggered by using the `Ext.Msg` singleton object, which is of class `Ext.MessageBox` class. This class exposes three methods, all sharing the same names with the equivalent browser based message boxes:

- `alert()`, which displays a title, a text and an OK button to dismiss the dialog
- `confirm()`, which prompts the user to answer a single question by "Yes" or "No"
- `prompt()`, which can be used to ask the user for some input

These dialog boxes are asynchronous

In spite of sharing the same name as their "native" JavaScript counterparts, the dialog boxes exposed by the Ext.Msg singleton object are asynchronous; this has several consequences:

1. The execution of the calling JavaScript code is not blocked until the user dismisses the dialog boxes, which in turn means that any network callbacks or other events are still being processed and executed.

2. To retrieve the input from the user, whenever any of these dialog boxes are dismissed, you have to provide a callback function that will be executed as soon as the user taps any of the buttons provided.

The following source code shows how to create a simple user interface with three buttons, each triggering a different kind of dialog box. The result of calling the Ext.Msg.alert() function can be seen in Figure 3-18.

```
items: [{
    xtype: 'button',
    text: 'alert()',
    itemId: 'alertButton',
    listeners: {
        tap: function (button, e, eOpts) {
            Ext.Msg.alert('alert()', 'This is an alert box');
        }
    }
}, {
    xtype: 'button',
    text: 'confirm()',
    itemId: 'confirmButton',
    listeners: {
        tap: function (button, e, eOpts) {
            Ext.Msg.confirm('confirm()', 'This is a confirm dialog', function
(answer) {
                Ext.Msg.alert('Answer to confirm()', 'You said ' + answer);
                console.log('Answer to confirm(): ' + answer);
            }, this);
        }
    }
}, {
    xtype: 'button',
    text: 'prompt()',
    itemId: 'promptButton',
    listeners: {
        tap: function (button, e, eOpts) {
            Ext.Msg.prompt('prompt()', 'This is a prompt dialog',
            function (answer, text) {
```

```
                    Ext.Msg.alert('Answer to prompt()', 'You said "' + text + '"');
                    console.log('Answer to prompt(): ' + text);
                }, this);
            }
        }
    }]
```

Figure 3-18. Alert dialog box

Picker

Pickers allow users of touchscreen devices to select an option from a set; the following code shows how to create a picker and then retrieve the choice back in the flow of the code, as shown in Figure 3-19.

```
{
    xtype: 'button',
    text: 'Touch to show picker',
```

```
listeners: {
    tap: function (button, e, eOpts) {
        if (!button.picker) {
            button.picker = Ext.widget('picker', {
                slots: [{ // ❶
                    name: 'first_name',
                    title: 'First name',
                    data: [{
                        text: 'John', value: 'john'
                    }, {
                        text: 'James', value: 'james'
                    }, {
                        text: 'Paul', value: 'paul'
                    }, {
                        text: 'Michael', value: 'michael'
                    }]
                }, {
                    name: 'last_name',
                    title: 'Last name',
                    data: [{
                        text: 'Smith', value: 'smith'
                    }, {
                        text: 'Raymond', value: 'raymond'
                    }, {
                        text: 'Graham', value: 'graham'
                    }, {
                        text: 'Fowler', value: 'fowler'
                    }]
                }],
                listeners: {    // ❷
                    cancel: function (picker, opts) {
                        Ext.Msg.alert('cancel', 'Picker has been canceled');
                    },
                    change: function (picker, value, opts) {
                            Ext.Msg.alert('chance', 'Picker has value: ' +
Ext.JSON.encode(value));
                    }
                }
            });
            Ext.Viewport.add(button.picker); // ❸
        }
        button.picker.show(); // ❹
    }
}
}]
```

❶ The slots configuration option is used to specify the items to be displayed in each of the "cylinders" of the component; each of the entries in the slots configuration must have a name, a title, and some data to display. The data is just an array of text/value pairs, each providing a human-readable and a computer-readable version of the information being displayed.

❷ The most important events of pickers are the cancel and the change events, which are self-explanatory. The change event handler function takes a value parameter, which is a simple dictionary with a sequence of key-value pairs. In this example we are just encoding it as a JSON text, to be displayed in a message box.

❸ Just like with any other panel, remember to add them to the Viewport prior to use!

❹ Use the show() function to display the picker.

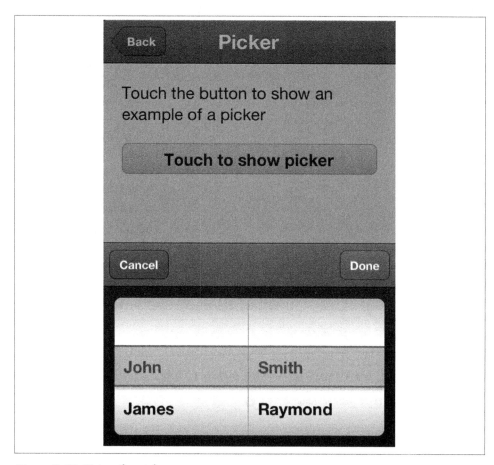

Figure 3-19. Using the picker

Sheet

The `Ext.Sheet` class (xtype `sheet`) provides a generic panel that appears animated on the screen and can display any kind of content. It is the base class of the `Ext.Action Sheet` class previously described.

This is a very simple code that shows how to create and display a `sheet` in a Sencha Touch application:

```
{
    xtype: 'button',
    text: 'Touch to show sheet',
    itemId: 'openButton',
    listeners: {
        tap: function (button, e, eOpts) {
            if (!button.sheet) {
                button.sheet = Ext.widget('sheet', {
                    html: 'Some text inside of the sheet',
                    style: 'color: white; font-weight: bold',
                    stretchX: true, // ❶
                    hideOnMaskTap: true
                });
                Ext.Viewport.add(button.sheet);
            }
            button.sheet.show();
        }
    }
}
```

❶   This parameter makes the sheet appear at the top of the application, next to the status bar. Otherwise, the sheet appears by default from the bottom, animating itself until it reaches the center of the screen.

Multimedia Views

Sencha Touch components are also able to display more than just buttons and data; several classes allow developers to include rich content into their applications, namely:

- Images
- Audio
- Video
- Charts
- Maps

We are going to learn more about each of these views in detail in the following sections.

Image

The Ext.Image class (xtype image) allows the placement in applications of individual images, just like the <img> tag allows it in standard HTML.

```
{
    xtype: 'image',
    src: '/img/icons/Icon@2x.png',
    height: 114,
    width: 114
}
```

The code will display an image, just like any other component, in your application (see Figure 3-20).

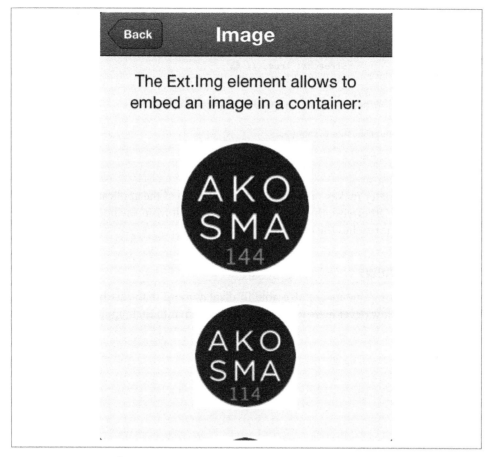

Figure 3-20. Using the Ext.Image class

Audio

The Ext.Audio class (xtype audio) wraps the HTML5 <audio> tag, supported by most major mobile web browsers these days. The configuration and the creation of a new instance of this class are straightforward, and the result is shown in Figure 3-21:

```
{
    xtype: 'audio',
    url  : 'res/audio/music.mp3'
}
```

The supported formats for audio are the following:

- Uncompressed WAV and AIF audio
- MP3 audio
- AAC-LC
- HE-AAC audio

 When used in Android devices, the audio tag does not provide native playback controls like in iOS; developers should then provide their own controls, and use the play(), pause(), stop(), and toggle() methods provided by the Ext.Media class instead.

Figure 3-21. Embedded audio

Video

Similarly to the audio element, the Ext.Video class (xtype video) can be used to wrap the native <video> tag provided by HTML5 in most major mobile web browsers.

```
{
    xtype: 'video',
    itemId: 'videoComponent',
    url  : 'res/video/iphone.m4v',
    posterUrl: 'res/video/jerome.png'
}
```

The code will yield an embedded video player as shown in Figure 3-22, with an image that is displayed while the video finishes loading (specified by the `posterUrl` property.)

> Just like with the `Ext.Audio` class, you must pay attention to the video formats supported in each platform; unfortunately, iOS and Android have different requirements, so it is very important to read the documentation in each case and to provide the formats that are supported in each case.
>
> Moreover, many older Android devices have known issues with video playback, which means that testing is required to make sure that the application behaves correctly in the supported devices for your application.

Figure 3-22. Embedded video

Charts

Sencha Touch 2 includes powerful 2D charting capabilities. As you have guessed, charts are represented by instances of the `Ext.chart.AbstractChart` class, of which three subclasses provide the most useful functionality:

- `Ext.chart.CartesianChart` (xtype `chart`) represents simple charts using the "x" and "y" Cartesian axes.

- `Ext.chart.PolarChart` (xtype `polar`) is used to display charts based on polar or radial coordinates.

- Ext.chart.SpaceFillingChart (xtype spacefilling) useful to display charts (without axes) that take all the available space in the component.

Ext.draw.Component

Itself, the Ext.chart.AbstractChart class inherits from Ext.draw.Com ponent, itself a subclass of Ext.Container. The Ext.draw.Component, as the name implies, allows developers to draw any kind of object on the UI of their applications. The Ext.draw.Component class is beyond the scope of this book, but suffice it to say that it wraps the Scalable Vector Graphics (SVG) and <canvas> functionality of the underlying browser, allowing an application to render any kind of visual content on the screen.

Charts in Sencha Touch are complex enough to deserve a whole chapter for themselves. In this book, we are just going to scratch the surface, showing how to create simple charts.

Charts are a commercial component of Sencha Touch

Although available in the GPL version of Sencha Touch, all the charts created with this version contain a watermark specifying that they were "Powered by Sencha Touch GPL." To remove this watermark, developers should get a commercial license for Sencha Touch.

One of the great features of Sencha Touch charts is that they are fully integrated with the data subsystem of the framework. Please refer to Chapter 4 for more information about the data management features of Sencha Touch.

To create a simple chart, you have to specify the following configuration options:

- store: Specifies the store that contains the data to be displayed. In the following example, the data will be retrieved from the JSONP API provided for free by open-weathermap.org (*http://openweathermap.org/data/2.1/history/station/39276? type=day*).
- series: Specifies the different series of data to be displayed in the chart. In the example that follows, we are displaying a line series, with the time in the x-axis, and the temperature in the y-axis.
- axes: This configuration option specifies the formatting and layout of each one of the axes in the chart: colors, labels, marks, etc.

- legend: Includes all the required information to format the legend of the chart correctly.

The following code shows an example of the configuration for a simple chart:

```
Ext.define('Chapter3Views.view.ChartsDemo', {
    extend: 'Ext.Container',
    xtype: 'chartsdemo',
    config: {
        layout: {
            type: 'fit'
        },
        items: [{
            xtype: 'chart', background: 'none',
            store: 'TemperatureStore', animate: true,
            interactions: ['panzoom', 'itemhighlight'],
            legend: {
                position: "bottom"
            },
            series: [{
                type: 'line', xField: 'time',
                yField: 'temperature', title: 'Temperatures',
                style: {
                    stroke: 'magenta', lineWidth: 2
                },
                highlightCfg: {
                    scale: 2
                },
                marker: {
                    type: 'circle', stroke: 'magenta',
                    fill: 'pink', lineWidth: 1,
                    radius: 3, shadowColor: 'rgba(0,0,0,0.7)',
                    shadowBlur: 10, shadowOffsetX: 3,
                    shadowOffsetY: 3,
                    fx: {
                        duration: 100
                    }
                }
            }],
            axes: [{
                type: 'numeric', position: 'left',
                grid: {
                    odd: {
                        fill: 'lightgray'
                    }
                },
                minZoom: 0.5, maxZoom: 2,
                style: {
                    axisLine: true,
                    stroke: 'lightgray'
                }
            }, {
```

```
            type: 'time', dateFormat: 'd M', position: 'bottom',
            minZoom: 0.5, maxZoom: 2,
            style: {
                stroke: 'lightgray'
            },
            label: {
                rotate: {
                    degrees: 315
                }
            }
        }]
    }]
    }
});
```

The result of the preceding code can be seen in Figure 3-23.

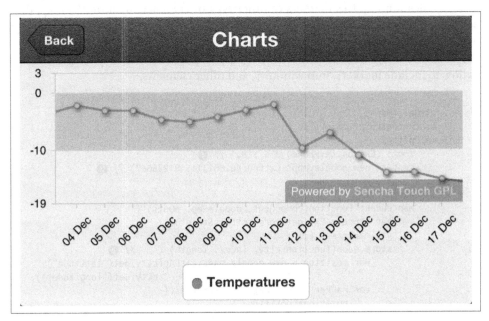

Figure 3-23. Charts

Map

The final type of multimedia view that we are going to discuss in this chapter is maps; Sencha Touch wraps the Google Maps API, allowing developers to include any kind of maps in their applications.

```
<script type="text/javascript"
src="http://maps.google.com/maps/api/js?sensor=true"></script>
```

Once the standard Google Maps API JavaScript file is included, adding a map view to a Sencha Touch application is a very simple task:

```
Ext.define('Chapter3Views.view.MapDemo', {
    extend: 'Ext.Panel',
    xtype: 'mapdemo',
    config: {
        layout: {
            type: 'card'
        },
        items: [{
            xtype: 'map',
            useCurrentLocation: true
        }]
    }
});
```

If the application requires markers or other type of embellishment on the map, then developers must use the standard markers API provided by Google. Sencha Touch does not provide any wrapper functionality to simplify this task. The following example shows how to integrate the Sencha Touch map component with other libraries, as well as how to include markers, info windows, and other elements.

```
{
    xtype: 'map',
    useCurrentLocation: false,
    mapOptions: {
        zoom: (Ext.os.is.Phone) ? 6 : 8,  // ❶
        center: new google.maps.LatLng(46.801111, 8.226667) // ❷
    },
    listeners: {
        maprender: function(component, googleMap, eOpts) {
            var store = Ext.getStore('citiesStore');
            var markers = [];
            store.each(function(city, index, length) {     // ❸
                var position = new google.maps.LatLng(city.get("latitude"),
                                                      city.get("longitude"));
                var marker = new google.maps.Marker({
                    position: position,
                    city: city
                });
                marker.setClickable(true);
                markers.push(marker);

                google.maps.event.addListener(marker, 'mouseup', function() {
                    var city = this.city;
                    var content = '<span style="font-weight: bold">'
                                    + city.get('name') + '</span>';
                    if (!component.infoWindow) {
                        component.infoWindow = new google.maps.InfoWindow(); // ❹
                    }
                    component.infoWindow.setContent(content);
```

```
        component.infoWindow.open(googleMap, this);
    });
});
var mcOptions = { gridSize: 50, maxZoom: 16 };
var markerCluster = new MarkerClusterer(googleMap, markers,
mcOptions); // ❺
    }
  }
}
```

❶   If the user is seeing this application in a smartphone, we use a smaller zoom factor than if using, say, a tablet or a desktop browser.

❷   This is the geographical center of Switzerland, according to Wikipedia (*http:// en.wikipedia.org/wiki/Geographical_centre_of_Switzerland*).

❸   For each city in the store, we are going to add a marker; as you can see, we are using the official marker API provided by Google, and not a Sencha Touch wrapper.

❹   We are creating a single InfoWindow object that will be shown every time the user taps on a marker. In this case we are attaching the function to the mouseup event, which at the time of this writing is the preferred way to do this and have a touchscreen-compatible behavior.

❺   This code uses the MarkerClusterer for Google Maps v3 library (*http://google-maps-utility-library-v3.googlecode.com/svn/trunk/markerclusterer/docs/refer ence.html*).

The result of this code is shown in Figure 3-24.[1]

Creating Views

The class model of Sencha Touch allows developers to create their own components, containers, or panels to satisfy the requirements of individual applications.

In this section, we are going to learn how to create the AkoLib.view.SplitView container class, provided as an example in the Github (*https://github.com/akosma/Sencha-Touch-2-Up-And-Running*) repository for this book. This class provides the following functionality:

• It is a subclass of Ext.Container and as such can contain other components inside.

---

1. The latitudes and longitudes of cities in Switzerland have been borrowed from timegenie.com (*http:// www.timegenie.com/latitude_and_longitude/country_coordinates/ch*).

- It provides a very similar user experience to the `UISplitViewController` class in iOS, allowing developers to create "master-detail" user interfaces in tablets and desktop applications.

 The full code of the `SplitView` class is available in the `AkoLib` folder of the source code distribution for this book, in Github (*https://github.com/akosma/Sencha-Touch-2-Up-And-Running*).

Figure 3-24. Google Maps

Choosing a Base Class

As we have seen, UI components in Sencha Touch can usually be grouped in the following families:

- Components
- Containers
- Panels

When faced with the creation of a new visual element, developers should ask themselves some very simple questions to find the proper base class to extend:

1. Should the new widget appear floating or on top of other components? If so, it should extend `Ext.Panel`. If not, continue to question 2.
2. Should the new widget contain other components? If so, then it should be a subclass of `Ext.Container`.
3. If the answer to both the previous questions is "no," then your new component should just extend `Ext.Component`.

In the case of the `AkoLib.view.SplitView` class, the answers for the questions are the following:

1. No.
2. Yes.

And thus it extends `Ext.Container`.

Creating the Class Skeleton

With the information at hand, we can begin the creation process of our own component; the file will be located in the `AkoLib/view` folder and will be named `SplitView.js`:

```
Ext.define('AkoLib.view.SplitView', {
    extend: 'Ext.Container',
    xtype: 'akosplitview',
    config: {},
    initialize: function () {
        this.callParent(arguments);
    }
});
```

The first elements of our new class are already in place:

- The `extend` attribute correctly specifies the base class of our new component.

- The xtype attribute provides a short name for our class so that instantiating it in our applications will be simpler and easier.

- The config attribute will hold several default values, many of which will be overridden by developers when using the class.

- The initialize function will allow us to customize the behavior and the properties of instances of this class in advanced ways.

The initialize function

As shown, the first thing to do every time you override a function provided by Sencha Touch is to call this.callParent(arguments), so that the behavior provided by the base class is executed before your own. Doing so ensures that every instance behaves in a predictable way.

Adding Configuration Options

We are going to add some configuration options to our component, all of which are completely customizable by developers using it:

```
Ext.define('AkoLib.view.SplitView', {
    extend: 'Ext.Container',
    xtype: 'akosplitview',
    config: {
        // Custom properties
        masterView: null,
        detailView: null,
        screenTitle: 'Sample Split View',
        menuButtonTitle: 'Menu',
        detailToolbarButtons: null,
        collapsesMasterView: null,
        showToggleButton: false,
        collapsed: false,

        // Common properties for components
        itemId: 'splitView',
        layout: 'hbox',
        items: []
    },
    initialize: function () {
        this.callParent(arguments);
    }
});
```

As you can see, configuration options can be of any type of object provided by JavaScript: Booleans, strings, numbers, or null values. Even better, every time a configuration option is defined in a new class, Sencha Touch automatically generates the corresponding setter and getter functions. For example, for our `masterView` configuration property, the class will provide `setMasterView()` and `getMasterView()` functions.

We also specify some common configuration options, such as `itemId`, `layout`, and `items`.

About setting the itemId

As shown in the example, we are not specifying the `id` property, but rather the `itemId` property. The distinction between those two is important, as Sencha Touch requires the `id` property to any two objects in an application to be strictly different. Using the `itemId` property in your own components ensures that Sencha Touch is able to generate different ID values for different instances of the same class.

In the case of the `AkoLib.view.SplitView` class, this is not a big deal, since there will usually be only one instance of it at any given time; however, for other component types, this is a critical consideration.

Providing Initialization

Whenever a new instance of this component is created, we want to set some event handlers that cannot be set using standard configuration options; we are going to use the `initialize()` function for that:

```
initialize: function(){
    this.callParent(arguments);

    var o = Ext.Viewport.getOrientation();
    this.handleOrientationChange({ orientation: o });
    Ext.Viewport.onBefore('orientationchange',
    'handleOnBeforeOrientationChange', this, { buffer: 50 });
        Ext.Viewport.on('orientationchange', 'handleOrientationChange', this,
{ buffer: 50 });

    // ...

    var showMenuButton = this.getShowMenuButton();
    showMenuButton.setText(this.getMenuButtonTitle());
    showMenuButton.addListener('tap', function (button, e, eOpts) {
        this.getOverlayView().showBy(button, 'tl-bc');
    }, this);

    // ...
}
```

The first thing that we want our `SplitView` component to do is to react to orientation changes; for that, we hook the `handleOrientationChange` function to the `orientation` change event, and then we use several getters and setters to build our user interface accordingly.

The event handlers handleOnBeforeOrietationChange, handleOrientationChange, and toggle are defined later on, as instance methods, as shown here:

```
Ext.define('AkoLib.view.SplitView', {
    extend: 'Ext.Container',
    xtype: 'akosplitview',
    config: {
        // ...
    },
    initialize: function () {
        this.callParent(arguments);
        // ...
    },

    handleOnBeforeOrientationChange: function () {
        // ...
    },
    handleOrientationChange: function (obj) {
        // ...
    },
    toggle: function () {
        // ...
    }
});
```

Firing Custom Events

The AkoLib.view.SplitView component has some interesting characteristics; it can toggle its master view, which can happen as well when the device is set in portrait orientation. Similarly, in portrait view, an overlay view can be used to show this same master view if required. We would like to be able to notify our clients about these facts, and for that we are going to extend our class with some custom events.

Creating events is simply a matter of calling the fireEvent() function, passing the name of the event as the first parameter, and passing an optional list of parameters after that. Usually the first parameter of an event handler will be a reference to the object firing the event.

The following source code shows how to call the fireEvent() function inside our new component:

```
showMasterView: function () {
    this.fireEvent('beforemasterviewshow', this);
    this.getMasterPanel().show();
    this.getShowMenuButton().hide();
    this.getToggleButton().setIconCls('arrow_left');
    this.setCollapsed(false)
```

```
        this.fireEvent('masterviewshow', this);
    }
```

Applications using the `AkoLib.view.SplitView` class can hook themselves into this workflow, adding their own event handlers:

```
launch: function () {
    Ext.Viewport.add({
        xtype: 'akosplitview',
        screenTitle: 'Universal App',
        menuButtonTitle: 'Menu',
        masterView: {
            xtype: 'indexview'
        },
        detailView: {
            xtype: 'panel',
            html: 'Select an item in the menu'
        },
        showToggleButton: true,
        collapsesMasterView: true,
        listeners: {
            masterviewshow: function (splitview) {
                console.log('masterviewshow event handler');
            }
        }
    });
}
```

Implement Private Methods

Although JavaScript does not actually allow methods to be marked private or public, we are going to define a series of methods that will only be used internally by the class to properly manage its state; as an example, here is the `getOverlayView()` function, which is used to show the overlay panel that holds the master view when the application is shown in portrait mode:

```
getOverlayView: function () {
    if (!this.overlayView) {
        this.overlayView = Ext.Viewport.add({
            xtype: 'panel',
            layout: 'card',
            modal: true,
            hideOnMaskTap: true,
            width: 300,
            height: 600,
            hidden: true,
            hideAnimation: 'fadeOut',
            showAnimation: 'fadeIn'
        });
        this.overlayView.addListener('show', function () {
            this.getOverlayView().add(this.getMasterView());
```

```
        }, this);
        this.overlayView.addListener('hide', function () {
            this.getMasterPanel().add(this.getMasterView());
        }, this);
    }
    return this.overlayView;
}
```

Conclusion

This chapter has provided an overview of the most visible part of Sencha Touch: its extensive support for complex view hierarchies. Developers can use the classes already provided by Sencha Touch, but thanks to the ease of use of the class system, they can also create their own views from scratch.

## CHAPTER 4

Data

Sencha Touch provides an incredible support for data-bound applications. Whether the information is stored locally or on a remote server, the framework allows developers to quickly prototype and develop applications consuming complex data, in XML or JSON formats.

This chapter will provide an introduction to the basic concepts of data management in Sencha Touch apps. You'll learn in detail about stores and proxies, as well as about different data-bound controls such as lists and data views.

Model Classes

The basic component of data bound applications is, without doubt, the `Ext.data.Mod` `el` class. Every business component of a Sencha Touch application, like for example "customers," "orders," or "invoices," is represented in Sencha Touch as a subclass of the `Ext.data.Model` class.

Sample application

To explain the concepts of this chapter, we are going to use a generic MVC application that consumes data in JSON or XML format. The data is produced by a set of PHP files, reading a rather large MySQL database containing random contact information. Users can choose whether to load data in JSON or XML format. Figure 4-1 shows a screenshot of the application.

This PHP application is located in the `Chapter_04_Data/Server` folder of the source code files provided with book, available in Github (*https:// github.com/akosma/Sencha-Touch-2-Up-And-Running*).

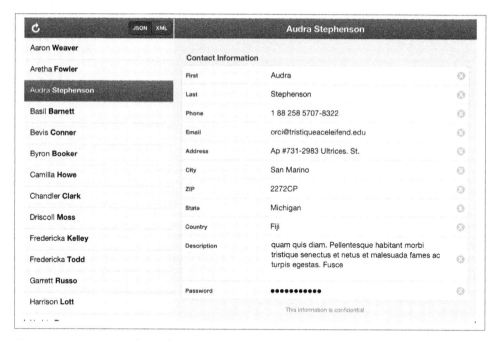

Figure 4-1. Data sample application

The following code provides the definition of a `Person` class:

```
Ext.define('Chapter4Data.model.Person', {
    extend: 'Ext.data.Model',
    config: {

        fields: [{
            name: 'entryId', type: 'int'
        }, {
            name: 'firstName', type: 'string'
        }, {
            name: 'lastName', type: 'string'
        }, {
//
// ... snip ...
//
        }, {
            name: 'enabled', type: 'boolean', defaultValue: true
        }, {
            name: 'createdOn',  type: 'date'
        }],

        idProperty: 'entryId',

        belongsTo: 'Company',
```

```
        hasMany: {
            model: 'Orders', name: 'orders'
        },

        validations: [{
            type: 'presence', field: 'firstName'
        }, {
            type: 'presence', field: 'lastName'
        }, {
            type: 'length', field: 'description', min: 15
        }, {
            type: 'inclusion', field: 'role', list: ['User', 'Admin']
        }]
    }
});
```

As previously shown, a model class definition consists of two major configuration options:

1. The list of the data fields that each instance of this class must store; they are represented as literal objects with name and type entries.

2. An idProperty entry, indicating the field that is used to uniquely identify each entry in a store. This field is extremely important, since as we are going to see in a minute, Sencha Touch stores use this information pervasively.

You can also specify other parameters together with the name and the type of a field; for example, developers can add information about default values using the defaultVal ue property; other useful properties are allowNull, sortDir (which can take the values ASC or DESC), or dateFormat (for date fields).

Finally, you can also specify model relationships, as well as validation logic in your models, which we'll learn more about in the following sections.

Model Field Types

Sencha Touch models can have fields with the following types:

- int
- string
- float
- boolean
- date

Every field in a model class is an instance of the Ext.data.Field class.

Associations

This is the part of the book where Ruby on Rails developers will feel at home. Sencha Touch allows us to define relationships among model classes, using two very common configuration properties: belongsTo and hasMany, which are self-explanatory.

Thanks to associations, developers can chain objects using these predefined semantics, creating code that is easy to read and which, thanks to stores and proxies, can be mapped to server-side entities as well:

```
var person = Ext.create('Chapter4Data.model.Person')
person.set('firstName', 'Aaron');
person.set('lastName', 'Schwartz');

var company = person.getCompany(function (company) {
    console.log('Here is the company information: ' + company.get('name'));
});

person.orders().add({
    item: 234,
    value: 699.00,
    note: 'To be delivered next month'
});

person.orders().sync();
```

The preceding script shows that the belongsTo relationship automatically generates a getCompany() function, which works asynchronously; you have to provide a callback to it, to be executed as soon as the data is retrieved. This is required to avoid blocking the JavaScript engine of the browser while the data is fetched, potentially from a remote location.

Validations

Finally, models can carry their own validation logic. Using the validations key in the configuration of a model, we can ensure that new instances are valid or not at any given time, providing a unified, simple API for developers.

There are many kinds of possible validations, all defined as functions in the Ext.data.Validations singleton object:

- email, used to check the proper formatting of email addresses
- inclusion and exclusion, which ensure that the value provided is included or not included in a predefined list
- format, making sure that a particular string conforms to some regular expression

- `length`, which as the name implies verifies the length of a particular string field

- `presence`, used to check the existence of a particular value in a model instance

During runtime, applications can use the `validate()` method on model instances to trigger all the required validations and to return an object containing all the information about any errors found during the procedure:

```
var person = Ext.create('Chapter4Data.model.Person')
person.set('firstName', 'Aaron');
person.set('lastName', 'Schwartz');

// Perform validation
var validationResults = person.validate();

console.log('Is valid? ' + validationResults.isValid());
console.log('All problems: ' + validationResults.items);
console.log('Specific problem: ' + validationResults.getByField('email'));
```

Stores and Proxies

Models, by themselves, are completely oblivious to any kind of storage mechanism; they just define in-memory individual data structures, with types, validation rules, and mutual interrelationships.

This is where stores and proxies come in; they provide ways to abstract different concepts that are pervasive in most data-bound apps, providing a plug-and-play API that isolates applications from the underlying data storage.

- **Stores** can be thought of as managed sets of model instances; for example, you can have a store containing all the instances of the `Person` class in your application. There are two basic types of stores: linear and hierarchical.

- **Proxies**, on the other hand, encapsulate the logic required to connect to a local or remote data source, such as the browser's `localStorage` object, or a REST web service elsewhere on the network.

There are two kinds of proxies available in Sencha Touch: local and remote. We are going to learn more about these two groups in the following sections.

Local Proxies

Local proxies are used by stores to keep sets of model instances in the local browser. There are three kinds of local proxies:

- Memory
- LocalStorage
- SessionStorage

Let's study each of these in detail.

Memory

The memory proxy, represented by the Ext.data.proxy.Memory class, is used only as a simple in-memory storage option that is not persisted across page refreshes.

The following code shows how to create a very simple memory proxy:

```
Ext.define('Chapter4Data.store.MemoryPeopleStore', {
    extend: 'Ext.data.Store',
    xtype: 'peoplestore',
    config: {
        model: 'Chapter4Data.model.Person',
        storeId: 'peopleStore',
        autoLoad: true,
        sorters: [{
            property: 'firstName',
            direction: 'ASC'
        }],
        proxy: {
            type: 'memory',
            reader: {
                type: 'json',
                root: 'people'
            }
        }
    }
});
```

You can use the Memory proxy to keep small amounts of in-memory temporary data. However, the SessionStorage proxy (described later in this section) is a better choice for larger quantities of temporary data.

LocalStorage

One of the most common proxies available in Sencha Touch is represented by the Ext.data.proxy.LocalStorage class, also identified by its localstorage xtype. This proxy uses the HTML5 localStorage functionality available in modern browsers, a simple key-value storage facility that accepts only strings for both keys and values. This proxy is able to serialize and deserialize complex objects into strings, transparently and seamlessly.

The code that follows shows a very simple example of a localstorage proxy:

```
Ext.define('Chapter4LocalStorage.store.PeopleStore', {
    extend: 'Ext.data.Store',
    xtype: 'peoplestore',
    config: {
        model: 'Chapter4LocalStorage.model.Person',
        storeId: 'peopleStore',
        autoLoad: true,
        autoSync: true,
        sorters: [{
            property: 'firstName',
            direction: 'ASC'
        }],
        proxy: {
            type: 'localstorage',
            id: 'peopleproxy'
        }
    }
});
```

The contents of the localStorage store are preserved across browser restarts, usually accepting a maximum of 5 MB of data. This might be the most useful local proxy available.

SessionStorage

Finally, the third local proxy available is the Ext.data.proxy.SessionStorage class, also identified by its xtype sessionstorage. This proxy uses the HTML5 sessionStorage functionality, which is very similar to the localStorage described in this chapter in terms of API. However, remember that the contents of the sessionStorage proxy are erased as soon as the browser window is closed; so in a certain way it is closer in behavior to the Memory proxy we have seen before.

The following code shows a very simple example of a sessionstorage proxy:

```
Ext.define('Chapter4LocalStorage.store.SessionPeopleStore', {
    extend: 'Ext.data.Store',
    xtype: 'peoplestore',
    config: {
        model: 'Chapter4LocalStorage.model.Person',
        storeId: 'peopleStore',
        autoLoad: true,
        autoSync: true,
        sorters: [{
            property: 'firstName',
            direction: 'ASC'
```

```
        }],
        proxy: {
            type: 'sessionstorage',
            id: 'peopleproxy'
        }
    }
});
```

The `SessionStorage` proxy stores its contents in disk, which makes it a better option than the `Memory` proxy for storing large amounts of temporary data.

Remote Proxies

Remote proxies are used to connect stores to remote data sources, located elsewhere on the network. They encapsulate all the logic required to perform typical "CRUD" (create, read, update, delete) operations on stores, and to map those operations to their corresponding HTML requests.

The remote proxies available in Sencha Touch are the following:

- `Ajax`
- `JsonP`
- `Rest`

The following sections will provide some insight about these proxies.

Ajax

The `ajax` proxy, represented by the `Ext.data.proxy.Ajax` class, is used to access data sources located in the same domain as the Sencha Touch application. This proxy encapsulates requests performed using the `XMLHTTPRequest` component, available in all modern browsers, and allowing developers to perform asynchronous HTTP requests from a web page.

Same domain policy

Remember that browsers are bound to the "same domain policy"; this limits the use of the `Ext.data.proxy.Ajax` proxy to web services located in the same domain as your Sencha Touch application.

The following code shows how to create a store using a very simple `ajax` proxy:

```
Ext.define('Chapter4Data.store.PeopleStore', {
    extend: 'Ext.data.Store',
    xtype: 'peoplestore',
    config: {
```

```
        model: 'Chapter4Data.model.Person',
        storeId: 'peopleStore',
        autoLoad: true,
        sorters: [{
            property: 'firstName',
            direction: 'ASC'
        }],
        proxy: {
            type: 'ajax',
            url : 'Server/index.php?format=json'
        }
    }
});
```

By default, `ajax` proxies can read data in JSON format; however, they can very easily read XML data as well, and for that, developers only need to specify a reader of type `Ext.data.reader.Xml`, whose xtype is simply `xml`:

```
{
    type: 'ajax',
    url : 'Server/index.php?format=xml',
    reader: {
        type: 'xml',
        rootProperty: 'data',
        record: 'person'
    }
}
```

As previously shown, the `xml` reader requires you to specify the `rootProperty` and the `record` properties; in this case, the values are `data` and `person` respectively, because the XML feed being read has the following structure:

```
<data>
    <person>
        <entryId>1857</entryId>
        <firstName>Jennifer</firstName>
        <lastName>Hudson</lastName>
        <phone>1 66 871 1728-5906</phone>
        <email>est.arcu.ac@sem.edu</email>
        <address>7509 Eleifend. Rd.</address>
        <city>Hope</city>
        <zip>A5C 9Z5</zip>
        <state>Gld.</state>
        <country>Mexico</country>
        <description>
            dui, semper et, lacinia vitae, sodales at, velit.
        </description>
        <password>FAB39FTL9MV</password>
        <createdOn>2010-07-25</createdOn>
        <modifiedOn>2009-12-19</modifiedOn>
    </person>
    <person>
```

```
        <!-- ... -->
    </person>
</data>
```

JsonP

To overcome the same-domain policy of the ajax proxy, the Ext.data.proxy.JsonP proxy class (usually referred to as jsonp) can be used. When this proxy is activated, it injects a <script> tag to the current DOM, with its src attribute pointing to the remote URL of the data service.

 The name JsonP comes from the expression "JSON with Padding," because the data served by the remote URL is "padded" with a function call, which enables it to be "activated" and consumed by the current JavaScript application.

The biggest limitation of this proxy is that it can execute only GET requests; however, they can be executed on any remote domain, not only on the current domain of the web application. The following code shows a simple example of how to create a jsonp proxy connecting to Twitter, in order to get the latest tweets about "argentina," for example:

```
{
    type: 'jsonp',
    url : 'http://search.twitter.com/search.json?q=argentina',
    reader: {
        type: 'json',
        rootProperty: 'results'
    }
}
```

Rest

The final remote proxy we are going to learn about is the rest proxy type, which is represented by the Ext.data.proxy.Rest class. This is a subclass of the Ext.data.proxy.Ajax class (which means that it can work only under the umbrella of the same-domain policy) and provides a means to easily connect to REST web services.

REST web services

REST stands for "REpresentational State Transfer" and is currently one of the strongest alternatives to Simple Object Access Protocol (SOAP) web services. Many server-side technologies allow developers to create REST web services, returning different kinds of data in formats such as XML and JSON; to name a few, Ruby on Rails, ASP.NET MVC, or even some PHP frameworks allow developers to create such services very easily.

The rest proxy can be configured to perform requests using different HTTP verbs for every CRUD operation:

- Create: POST
- Read: GET
- Update: PUT
- Delete: DELETE

REST proxies can also be configured, through the api property, to use different URLs for each of these operations, if required by the server-side technology being used.

The following code snippet shows the creation of a very simple rest proxy attached directly to a model.

```
Ext.define('Chapter4Data.model.Person', {
    extend: 'Ext.data.Model',
    config: {
        fields: [{
            name: 'id',
            type: int
        }, {
            // ... snip ...
        }],

        proxy: {
            type: 'rest',
            url: '/users'
        }
    }
});
```

Once a model has been defined this way, you can manipulate its instances directly in your controllers and just use the save() method, which will automatically push any changes to the remote web server automatically:

```
var person = Ext.create('Chapter4Data.model.Person', {
    firstName: 'John',
```

```
        lastName: 'Smith'
});

// This will trigger a POST request to "/users"
person.save({
    success: function (person) {
        console.log('new person has been sent to the server!');
    }
});
```

The dictionary passed to the save() function includes a set of optional callbacks to be executed asynchronously as soon as the network operation completes.

 What about SOAP web services?
Many companies have invested heavily in web services using the SOAP technology, which received a strong push by Microsoft and other vendors in the early 2000s. To help these companies leverage the power of the platform, the Sencha team has announced the availability of a SOAP proxy (*http://www.sencha.com/blog/taking-a-look-at-the-new-sencha-soap-data-proxy*), but (at least at the moment of this writing) it is only available to companies and teams who have purchased a "Sencha Complete: Team" package. Also, it is only available for desktop applications developed with Ext JS 4.1.2.

Store Types

While proxies encapsulate the logic required to read and write information, stores are designed to hold data and to make it available to other components, most notably data-bound components such as lists.

The two most common kinds of stores are linear ones, usually just referred to as stores, and hierarchical stores, usually represented by tree stores. We are going to learn more about these two kinds of stores in the following sections.

The StoreManager Singleton

Sencha Touch MVC applications usually contain one or more stores, and they are usually referred to from different locations: event handlers, controllers, or even from the Ext.application() function call.

To make it easier for developers to work with several stores in the same application, and to be able to refer uniquely to each one of them, the Ext.data.StoreManager singleton comes in handy. It provides a simple lookup() method which takes an ID as parameter; this ID must be a string, and it is the same one provided in the storeId configuration property.

For convenience, the `Ext.data.StoreManager.lookup()` function is aliased to `Ext.get Store()`, which is a commonly used alternative, particularly in the code samples for this book.

Linear stores

The most common kind of store is the linear one, usually represented by an instance of the `Ext.data.Store` class. In the grand scheme of a Sencha Touch MVC application, stores are associated to a model, and stores contain a proxy object. Proxies are usually associated with a **Reader** and a **Writer** object, which contain the logic required to serialize back and forth model objects from the transport mechanism used.

Let's take a look at a simple example of a store and a proxy.

```
Ext.define('Chapter4Data.store.PeopleStore', {
    extend: 'Ext.data.Store',
    xtype: 'peoplestore',
    config: {
        model: 'Chapter4Data.model.Person',
        storeId: 'peopleStore',
        autoLoad: true,
        sorters: [{
            property: 'firstName',
            direction: 'ASC'
        }],
        proxy: {
            type: 'ajax',
            url : 'Server/index.php?format=json'
        }
    }
});
```

In the preceding code, we define a class named `Chapter4Data.store.PeopleStore` which is associated to the `Person` model we have defined previously. We also define some key properties of our store:

- `storeId` provides a unique string that can be used to retrieve this store instance from anywhere in the application, using `Ext.data.StoreManager.lookup()` or its alias `Ext.getStore()`.

- `autoLoad` specifies that as soon as this object is created and initialized, it will attempt to connect to the remote (or local) data source automatically. There is a similar property called `autoSync` that can be used to push back to the proxy object any changes that have been made in the store at runtime.

- `sorters` provides the information required to sort the information on the store automatically.

- Finally, `proxy` contains the definition of the proxy object associated to the store. In this case, it's an `ajax` kind of proxy, whose `url` is specified immediately after.

One of the most interesting characteristics of the association between stores and proxies is that they can be composed at runtime; a store can change its proxy dynamically, and thus "talk" to a different server or storage mechanism as required; in the following code we see such a behavior taking place.

```
switchFormat: function (segmentedButton, button, isPressed, eOpts) {
    // Get a reference to the store
    var store = Ext.getStore('peopleStore');

    // This is required because the "Ext.SegmentedButton" class
    // calls its event handler once for each button; we are only
    // interested in the event pertaining to the pressed button:
    if (isPressed) {
        var format = button.getText();
        var newProxy = null;

        // If the user selects "JSON," use an AJAX proxy
        // with a JSON reader (the default option)
        if (format === 'JSON') {
            newProxy = {
                type: 'ajax',
                url : 'Server/index.php?format=json'
            };
        }

        // Otherwise, use an XML reader
        else if (format === 'XML') {
            newProxy = {
                type: 'ajax',
                url : 'Server/index.php?format=xml',
                reader: {
                    type: 'xml',
                    rootProperty: 'data',
                    record: 'person'
                }
            };
        }

        // Set the proxy in the store and reload!
        store.setProxy(newProxy);
        store.load();
    }
}
```

Object composition at work!

Hierarchical stores

The other kind of store is the hierarchical store, usually represented by an instance of the `Ext.data.TreeStore` class, whose xtype is `tree`.

Tree stores have their origin in the ExtJS framework, where they are used to represent visual tree nodes in UI widgets; however, given that Sencha Touch is a touchscreen framework, and that common tree-like UIs are hard to represent and manipulate with fingers, tree stores are usually associated with the `Ext.dataview.NestedList` class, which will be described in detail.

For the moment, suffice to show the following tree store definition:

```
store: {
    type: 'tree',
    fields: [{                        // ❶
        name: 'text',
        type: 'string'
    }],
    defaultRootProperty: 'team',      // ❷
    sorters: 'text',                  // ❸
    root: {
        text: 'Teams',
        team: [{
            text: 'Finance',
            team: [{
                text: 'Alma Boyle',
                leaf: true
            }]                        // ❹
        }, {
            text: 'Accounting',
            team: [{
                text: 'Fletcher Herbert',
                leaf: true
            }, {
                text: 'Elmo Irwin',
                leaf: true
            }]
        }, {
            text: 'Human Resources',
            team: [{
                text: 'Felicia Gray',
                leaf: true
            }, {
                text: 'Petra Ferguson',
                leaf: true
            }]
        }]
    }
}
```

❶   Instead of defining a `model` property that points to some subclass of `Ext.da ta.Model`, we can simply specify the names (eventually also the types) of the fields of each data item.

❷   The `defaultRootProperty` specifies the name of the key, in each data node, that contains child items. If not specified, the tree store will use the value `children`.

❸   Specifying the `sorters` property here will automatically provide the store values in an ordered fashion.

❹   The `root` property contains the raw hierarchical data of each node. Pay attention to the fact that each node has both a `text` property (used for sorting and displaying) and a `teams` property, previously defined as the `defaultRootProper ty`.

We are going to see a detailed example of use of a `tree` store when learning about the `Ext.dataview.NestedList` class.

Data-Bound Controls

One of the most important uses of stores is to be paired to data-bound view components, such as a list. Whenever a data-bound component is shown on the screen, it associates in such a way to its store that any change in the underlying data will be reflected automatically in the visual component. Developers do not need to call any `refresh()` method to see their changes; as soon as a model instance is changed in the store, the associated view component is updated automatically.

The three data-bound controls available in Sencha Touch are the following:

- DataView
- List
- NestedList

We are going to learn more about these in the following sections.

DataView

The `Ext.dataview.DataView` class (also known by its xtype `dataview`) is the simplest of all the data-bound controls. It can be thought of as a very simple template engine, which takes data from a store as a parameter and renders that data according to a string template.

The following example shows a very simple `dataview` loading some tweets about Argentina:

```
Ext.define('Chapter4DataViews.view.DataViewDemo', {
    extend: 'Ext.dataview.DataView',
    xtype: 'dataviewdemo',
    config: {
        xtype: 'dataview',
        title: 'DataView Demo',
        itemTpl: '<div class="tweetdiv"><div class="avatar">
        <img src="{profile_image_url}" /></div><div class="text">
        <p class="username">{from_user_name}</p><p class="tweet">{text}
        </p><p class="date">{[Ext.Date.format(values.created_at, "d.m.Y, H:i")]}
        </p></div></div>', // ❶
        store: {
            autoLoad: true,
            fields: [{
                name: 'id', type: 'int'
            }, {
                name: 'profile_image_url', type: 'string'
            }, {
                name: 'from_user', type: 'string'
            }, {
                name: 'from_user_name', type: 'string'
            }, {
                name: 'text', type: 'string'
            }, {
                name: 'created_at', type: 'date',
                dateFormat: 'D, j M Y H:i:s O' // ❷
            }],
            proxy: {
                type: 'jsonp',
                url: 'http://search.twitter.com/search.json?q=argentina',
                // ❸
                reader: {
                    type: 'json',
                    rootProperty: 'results'
                }
            }
        }
    }
});
```

❶ The itemTpl property specifies a string or an Ext.XTemplate object, used to render each item in the data store. Pay attention to the fact that the data is formatted using the Ext.Date.format() function, inside the template code. Even mathematical expressions can be used in templates.

❷ Here we specify the format of each created_at field, as returned by Twitter. Sencha Touch will take care of transforming each one of these values into a proper JavaScript Date object for us.

❸ This store is attached to a very simple jsonp proxy, downloading the latest tweets about Argentina.

The itemTpl property provides a rather complex template, which can be styled as follows to get the result shown in Figure 4-2:

```
div.tweetdiv {
    float: left; width: 300px; padding: 10px 10px 0px 10px; margin: 10px;
    border-color: lightgray; border-width: 1px;
    border-style: solid; min-height: 150px;
}

div.avatar {
    float: left; width: 50px; margin-left: 10px;
    margin-right: 10px; margin-top: 5px;
}

div.text {
    width: 200px; float: left;
}

p.username {
    font-weight: bold; font-size: 0.8em;
}

p.tweet {
    margin-top: 5px; font-size: 0.8em;
}

p.date {
    color: gray; font-size: 0.7em; margin-top: 5px; margin-bottom: 10px;
}
```

This CSS code is stored in the Chapter_04_DataViews/css/styles.css file included in the source code of the book.

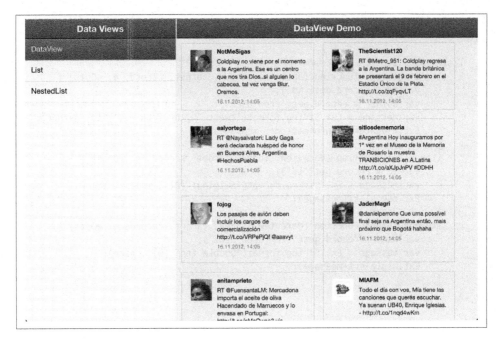

Figure 4-2. DataView on an iPad

DataView Events

As expected, the Ext.dataview.DataView class (and its subclasses) are able to react to various events; the most important are the following:

- itemtap and itemsingletap: They are both triggered when the user taps only once on any item of the dataview.
- itemdoubletap: Triggered when the user double-taps on an item.
- itemswipe: Executed when the user swipes his finger on top of a particular item.

itemtap versus itemsingletap

The main difference between itemtap and itemsingletap is that the former is triggered immediately, while the second one is triggered with a slight delay of a couple of milliseconds; thus, the itemsingletap event is specially adapted to be used together with the itemdoubletap event, because in case the user taps twice on an object, the itemtap event would not yield to the execution of the itemdoubletap event.

Using the `listeners` configuration key, we can add some event handlers for our data view:

```
listeners: {
    itemsingletap: function (dataview, index, target, record, e, eOpts) {
        var id = record.get('id');
        var author = record.get('from_user');
        var message = Ext.String.format('Tweet {0}<br>from {1}', id, author);
        Ext.Msg.alert('Information', message);
    },
    itemswipe: function (dataview, index, target, record, e, eOpts) {
        var id = record.get('id');
        var message = Ext.String.format('Swiping! {0}', id);
        Ext.Msg.alert(message);
    },
    itemdoubletap: function (dataview, index, target, record, e, eOpts) {
        var name = record.get('from_user_name');
        var message = Ext.String.format('Double tap! {0}', name);
        Ext.Msg.alert(message);
    }
}
```

Lists

Lists are the quintessential data-bound control. They are represented by the `Ext.data view.List` class, itself a subclass of `Ext.dataview.DataView`. Similarly as their superclass, they require a `store` definition (in this case, the `peoplestore` defined earlier in the chapter) and an `itemTpl` which defines the template used to render each cell of the list.

The code that follows describes a very simple list, attached to the `peoplestore` mentioned previously:

```
Ext.define('Chapter4DataViews.view.IndexView', {
    extend: 'Ext.navigation.View',
    xtype: 'indexview',
    config: {
        id: 'navigationView',
        items: [{
            xtype: 'list',
            title: 'People',
            store: {
                xtype: 'peoplestore'
            },
            itemTpl: '<div class="contact">{firstName} <strong>{lastName}
            </strong></div>'
        }]
    }
});
```

Lists can also be grouped, and they could also show a nice `indexBar` on the right side to simplify navigation and scrolling, and the result would be the same as shown in Figure 4-3:

```
{
    xtype: 'list',
    title: 'People',
    grouped: true,
    indexBar: true,
    store: {
        xtype: 'peoplestore'
    },
    itemTpl: '<div class="contact">{firstName} <strong>{lastName}
    </strong></div>'
}
```

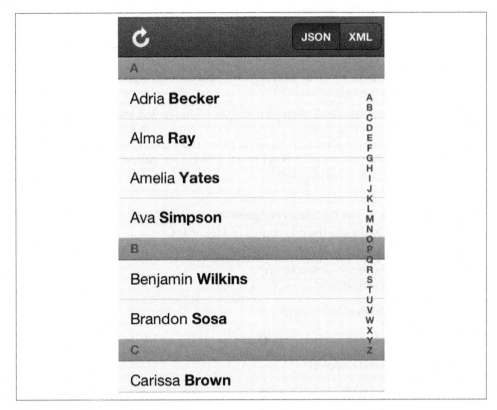

Figure 4-3. List component

Finally, just like their superclass, `list` components can react to the `itemtap`, `item swipe`, and `itemdoubletap` events. They can also react to the `disclose` event, which is fired when the user taps on the disclosure button.

Nested Lists

Finally, nested lists (represented by the `Ext.dataview.NestedList` component, whose xtype is `nestedlist`) are used to represent hierarchical stores, implemented using the `Ext.data.TreeStore` class seen previously in this chapter.

A `nestedlist` component does not inherit either from `Ext.dataview.DataView` or from `Ext.dataview.List`; rather, it is a class that uses as many `list` components as required to help the user navigate the hierarchy of data being presented.

Nested lists or navigation views?

The question has come from many different developers: When is it better to use a nested list versus a navigation view with a series of embedded list components?

The answer, as always in these cases, is the famous "It depends." Experience shows that nested lists are quite rigid and inflexible components, which usually work best when the underlying hierarchical data set is uniform and coherent. In those cases, nested lists are wonderfully simple and straightforward.

On the other hand, when your application has to deal with heterogeneous sets of data, where parents and children have radically different structures, or when each list has to have a really different visual layout from the rest, then it is better to use a navigation view, encapsulating individual consecutive lists.

The following code shows the basic configuration required to get a nested list in your application, which looks like the one shown in Figure 4-4:

```
Ext.define('Chapter4DataViews.view.NestedListDemo', {
    extend: 'Ext.dataview.NestedList',
    xtype: 'nestedlistdemo',
    config: {
        title: 'Teams',
        margin: 20,
        listConfig: {              // ❶
            ui: 'round',
            itemTpl: '{text}'
        },
        detailCard: {              // ❷
            xtype: 'panel',
            html: 'This is the leaf node detail card'
        },
        listeners: {               // ❸
            itemtap: function (nestedList, list, index,
            target, record, e, eOpts) {
                var name = record.get('text');
```

```
                    var html = Ext.String.format('This is the leaf
                    node card of {0}', name);
                    this.getDetailCard().setHtml(html);
                }
            },
            store: {                    // ❹
                // ...
            }
        }
    });
```

❶ The configuration of each list used by the nestedlist can be modified using the
    listConfig property. Ensure that the same configuration will be used for all the
    lists used by the nestedlist.

❷ The detailCard property (which can be accessed by event handlers using the
    getDetailCard() getter function) contains a panel definition, which is
    automatically displayed every time the user selects an item whose leaf flag is set
    to true.

❸ The listeners key, as usual, contains the definition of event handlers to be
    executed at some point in the future.

❹ Please refer to the previous section about stores, where we have shown how to
    create a hierarchical Ext.data.TreeStore object.

Figure 4-4. Nested list component

Different itemtap events handler signatures!

Pay attention to the fact that the `itemtap` event handler signature is different between the `Ext.dataview.NestedList` and the `Ext.data view.List` classes; for the `nestedlist` class, this is the signature:

```
itemtap(nestedList, list, index, target, record, e, eOpts)
```

while for the `list` and `dataview` classes, it's the following:

```
itemtap(list, index, target, record, e, eOpts)
```

This is due to the fact that `NestedList` "contains" an instance of the `List` class, and as such the event handler receives a pointer to both objects. This difference in signatures is often a source of confusion.

Conclusion

One of the most important aspects for enterprise applications is the management of data, and this is precisely one of the strongest points of Sencha Touch. It offers a complete set of tools to allow developers to describe not only data structures, including their validation rules and mutual interrelationships, but also the storage mechanisms that apply in each case, and it even proposes a set of visual components that automatically bind themselves to stores for displaying data.

## CHAPTER 5

Forms

Forms are a fundamental element to enable interactivity in data-driven business applications; Sencha Touch builds upon the latest features of HTML5 to provide advanced support for forms.

This chapter will describe in detail all the different types of fields that you can use in your forms, and how you can enable your mobile users to enter and modify data in your applications.

Form Panels

Forms in Sencha Touch have a very simple architecture: an instance of `Ext.form.Panel` holds one of many `Ext.form.Fieldset` instances, and each fieldset can contain one or more instances of any of the available subclasses of `Ext.field.Field`. (See Figure 5-1 for an example of Sencha Touch form structure.)

The available types of fields in Sencha Touch are described in Table 5-1, including their common class names and their xtypes.

Table 5-1. Sencha Touch form classes and xtypes

xtype	Class
fieldset	Ext.form.FieldSet
field	Ext.field.Field
checkboxfield	Ext.field.Checkbox
datepickerfield	Ext.field.DatePicker
emailfield	Ext.field.Email
hiddenfield	Ext.field.Hidden
numberfield	Ext.field.Number
passwordfield	Ext.field.Password
radiofield	Ext.field.Radio
searchfield	Ext.field.Search
selectfield	Ext.field.Select
sliderfield	Ext.field.Slider
spinnerfield	Ext.field.Spinner
textfield	Ext.field.Text
textareafield	Ext.field.TextArea
togglefield	Ext.field.Toggle
urlfield	Ext.field.Url

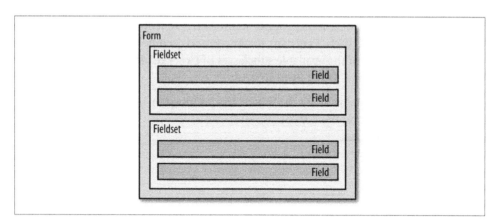

Figure 5-1. Sencha Touch form structure

Figure 5-2 shows the class hierarchy of the different types of fields available in Sencha Touch.

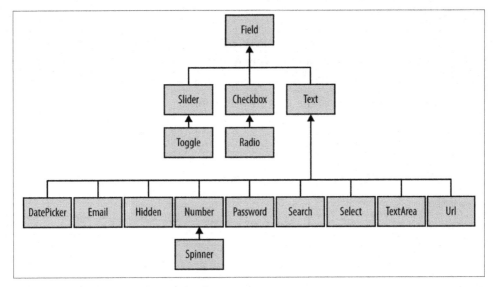

Figure 5-2. Field classes hierarchy diagram

Fieldsets

The fields of a form can be grouped visually inside an instance of the Ext.form.Field set class; a form can have as many fieldsets as required, of course, and they would appear one below the other following the order of their definition. You can create fieldsets by adding them to the items property of the enclosing form, using the fieldset xtype property.

Fieldsets have a few configuration properties:

- title provides descriptive text on top of the fields. This helps the user to figure out the roles of the different fieldsets.

- instructions provides longer text, appearing below the fields, with detailed information about the context and type of information expected in that section of the form.

Field Types

This section will provide an overview of the types of fields that are available in Sencha Touch.

Text Fields

Text fields are the most common and simple to use. The base `Text` field class provides lots of functionality, shared by all the types of text entry fields, such as capitalization, validation, events, and look and feel.

There are several subclasses of the `Text` field available:

- `DatePicker`
- `Email`
- `Hidden`
- `Number`
- `Password`
- `Search`
- `Select`
- `TextArea`
- `Url`

By default, all text fields share the following configuration options:

- `autoCapitalize`, `autoComplete`, and `autoCorrect` all take Boolean values, which activate and deactivate each one of the options.
- `clearIcon` makes the field display a small button, used to clear the current value of the field in a simple gesture.
- `maxLength` specifies the maximum length of text accepted by the current instance.
- `placeHolder` provides a text to be shown to the user when the field does not contain any information or contents. This is particularly useful as a help for users to learn which kind of information to enter into complex forms.
- `readOnly` is a Boolean value that specifies whether the current field can be modified by the user.

You can see all the text fields in action in Figure 5-3.

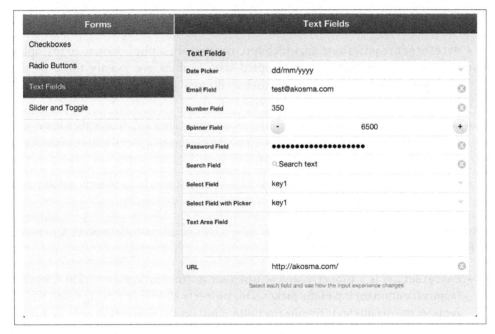

Forms		Text Fields	
Checkboxes		**Text Fields**	
Radio Buttons		Date Picker	dd/mm/yyyy
Text Fields		Email Field	test@akosma.com
Slider and Toggle		Number Field	350
		Spinner Field	- 6500 +
		Password Field	••••••••••••••••••••
		Search Field	⌕ Search text
		Select Field	key1
		Select Field with Picker	key1
		Text Area Field	
		URL	http://akosma.com/

Select each field and see how the input experience changes

Figure 5-3. Text fields in a form

We are going to study each one of them in detail in the next sections.

DatePicker

As the name implies, this component is meant to simplify the selection of a date or time in a form. The DatePicker component in Sencha Touch is heavily inspired by the date picker in iOS, using the visual idiom of scrolling wheels.

This component is quite characteristic in its structure: To select dates, an instance of the DatePicker field contains (does not inherit, but contains) an instance of the Ext.picker.Date class, which is in turn a subclass of Ext.picker.Picker, itself a subclass of Ext.Sheet. All of this explains that the DatePicker component shows up as a sheet, popping up from the bottom edge of the screen, all while displaying a slot-based picker.

When the user is not selecting dates, the DatePicker field appears like a normal field on screen, showing the date using a human-readable, configurable format.

 Please refer to Chapter 3 for a description of the Ext.picker.Picker class.

There are several configuration options available for the `DatePicker` field:

- `dateFormat` requires a string, which specifies the formatting option used to display the date on the picker. The accepted date formats are exactly those of the `Ext.Date.format()` function, themselves directly inspired by those of the PHP "date()" function (*http://www.php.net/date*).

- `value` specifies the default value of the picker upon creation. It accepts a variety of values, ranging from standard JavaScript `Date` objects to a literal object of the form `{year: 2012, day: 10, month: 9}`.

- `picker` is a getter that provides access to the `Ext.picker.Date` object contained by the current instance.

There are several available configuration options for `Ext.picker.Date` objects, to name a few:

- `cancelButton` is a property which, when set to true, makes the picker feature a "Cancel" button on top of the picker. This property also takes a string value, which replaces the default text. To hide the button, just set the property to `null` or `false`.

- `doneButton` is very similar to `cancelButton`, but when activated provides the user with a button that can be used to dismiss the picker and return the chosen date to the calling code.

- `height` specifies the height in points of the picker.

- `slotOrder` specifies the order of the day, month, and year slots in the picker; by default, the American English "month/day/year" structure is used, so specifying a value like `["day", "month", "year"]` will make your picker more familiar to European audiences.

- `yearFrom` and `yearTo` specify the upper and lower bounds for the year slots.

All of these properties are demonstrated in the following code sample:

```
{
    xtype: 'datepickerfield',
    name: 'date',
    label: 'Date Picker',
    dateFormat: 'D d M Y',
    placeHolder: 'dd/mm/yyyy',
    picker: {
        slotOrder: [ 'day', 'month', 'year' ],
        yearFrom: (new Date()).getFullYear(),
        yearTo: (new Date()).getFullYear() + 20
    }
}
```

The code above generates a date picker that looks like the one in Figure 5-4.

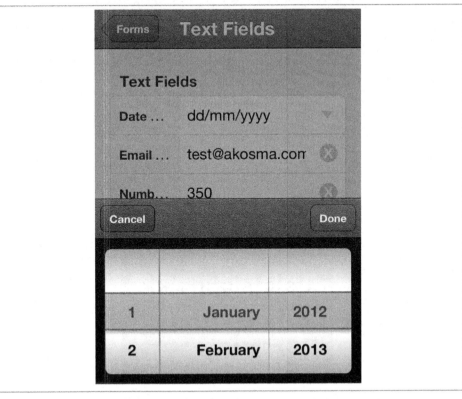

Figure 5-4. Date picker

Email

The `Email` field type encapsulates the creation of a standard HTML5 `<input type="email">` field. Recent mobile web browsers will show a specialized keyboard, suitable for typing email addresses with a touchscreen mobile device.

 To learn more about the different types of available HTML5 form fields, check out Mobile JavaScript Application Development (O'Reilly).

```
{
    xtype: 'emailfield',
    name: 'email',
    value: 'test@akosma.com',
    label: 'Email Field',
    required: false
}
```

You can see the keyboard associated to the email field in Figure 5-5.

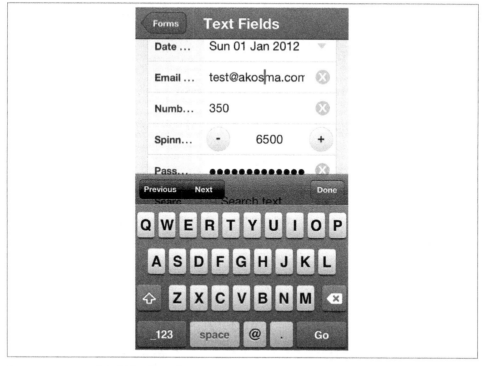

Figure 5-5. Email field keyboard

Hidden

This component just encapsulates the creation of a standard `<input type="hidden">`
HTML component, used to store values out of sight from the user.

```
{
    xtype: 'hiddenfield',
    name: 'hidden',
    value: 'Some invisible value',
    label: 'Hidden Field'
}
```

Number

This subclass of the Text field is used to provide an easy way for users to enter numeric
values; this includes displaying an ad hoc keyboard, suitable for number input, as well
as a set of spinner buttons to make the entry process even easier.

There are several possible configurations:

- `minValue` and `maxValue` provide the lower and upper bounds of the range of accepted values in the field.

- `stepValue` specifies the amount of change to be applied to the field every time the user taps on the spinner buttons.

```
{
    xtype: 'numberfield',
    name: 'number',
    value: '350',
    label: 'Number Field',
    minValue: 100,
    maxValue: 500,
    stepValue: 10
}
```

Spinner

This is a special kind of Number field, which displays a pair of buttons used to increment and decrement the value of the field, which simplifies the taks of the user to enter and modify values.

There are some configuration options particularly useful for this component:

- `accelerateOnTapHold` is `true` by default and specifies whether the user is able to accelerate the increase rate of the field if she keeps touching the same button.

- `cycle` is a Boolean (set to `false` by default) that makes the component return to the minimum value when the maximum value is reached, or to the maximum value as soon as the minimum value is reached.

- `increment` is the value that is subtracted or added to the component every time one of the spinner buttons is touched.

- `groupButtons` is a Boolean value (set to `true` by default) that specifies the relative position of the spinner buttons; when `true`, they appear together at the right side of the field; when `false`, they appear on each side of the input field.

```
{
    xtype: 'spinnerfield',
    name: 'spinner',
    value: '6500',
    label: 'Spinner Field',
    minValue: 1000,
    maxValue: 10000,
    stepValue: 10,
    accelerateOnTapHold: true,
    cycle: false,
    increment: 200,
```

```
        groupButtons: false
    }
```

Password

The `Password` field is used, as expected, to provide a concealed input field for the user to enter secure or sensitive data.

```
{
    xtype: 'passwordfield',
    name: 'password',
    value: 'Some secret password',
    label: 'Password Field'
}
```

Search

This special kind of `Text` input provides a typical search box, with rounded corners and a magnifying glass icon on the field.

```
{
    xtype: 'searchfield',
    name: 'search',
    value: 'Search text',
    label: 'Search Field'
}
```

Select

This component provides a touchscreen-enabled pop-up field, where the user can select one of many different predefined options. There are several configurations available beyond those of the `Text` field:

- `options` provides all the options to be displayed on the picker UI. These are usually represented as an array of literal objects with defined fields.

- `displayField` specifies the field that contains the text shown to the user.

- Similarly, `valueField` specifies the key of the `options` array objects to be used as machine-readable data, for submissions and other operations.

- `store` specifies the `Ext.data.Store` object to be used as data source for this component. This makes it easy to bind this component to a local or remote data source.

- `usePicker` is a Boolean value that toggles the component from using a list overlay (the default) to a standard `Ext.picker.Picker` object instead.

The following code snippet shows how to create a simple select field that uses a modal popover (visible only in the iPad or other tablets):

```
{
    xtype: 'selectfield',
    name: 'select',
    label: 'Select Field',
    options: [{
        display: 'key1',
        value: 'value1'
    }, {
        display: 'key2',
        value: 'value2'
    }, {
        display: 'key3',
        value: 'value3'
    }],
    displayField: 'display',
    valueField: 'value'
}
```

You can see the select field popover in Figure 5-6.

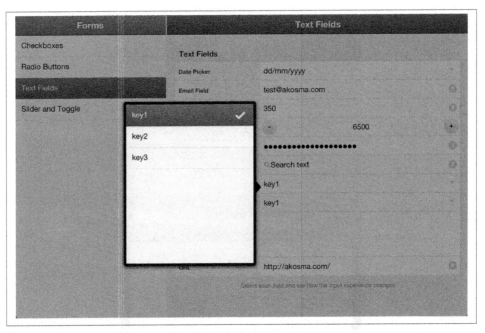

Figure 5-6. Modal popover for tablets

On the other hand, the following code shows the same example but using a standard picker:

```
{
    xtype: 'selectfield',
    name: 'select',
    label: 'Select Field with Picker',
    usePicker: true,
    options: [{
        display: 'key1',
        value: 'value1'
    }, {
        display: 'key2',
        value: 'value2'
    }, {
        display: 'key3',
        value: 'value3'
    }],
    displayField: 'display',
    valueField: 'value'
}
```

The standard picker used for select fields can be seen in Figure 5-7.

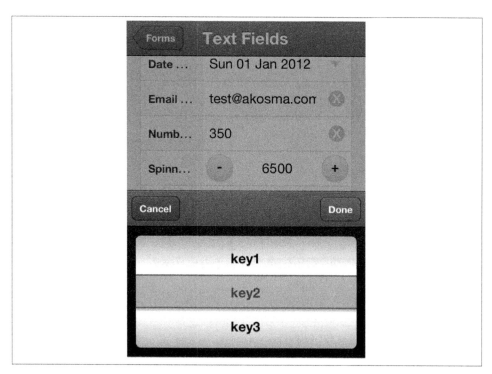

Figure 5-7. Standard picker for select fields

TextArea

This component provides a common multi-line entry field, suitable for entering longer quantities of text than usual text fields.

 Entering text in touchscreen devices is usually considered a tedious option, so use this component carefully.

There is a simple yet common configuration option for this component: maxRows, which takes an integer value specifying the maximum visible number of rows available for the user on screen.

```
{
    xtype: 'textareafield',
    name: 'textarea',
    label: 'Text Area Field'
}
```

Url

This last type of Text encapsulates the creation of an <input type="url"> HTML5 component, which allows users to conveniently type URLs. Modern touchscreen browsers provide an adapted keyboard for entering URL data into forms.

```
{
    xtype: 'urlfield',
    name: 'url',
    label: 'URL',
    value: 'http://akosma.com/'
}
```

You can see the keyboard associated with the URL field in Figure 5-8.

Figure 5-8. URL field keyboard

Checkboxes and Radio Groups

Checkboxes provide a very simple and standard UI for users, allowing them to answer "yes" or "no" to a simple question.

Checkboxes can be configured using the following properties:

- `name` provides the machine-readable name of the data to be checked or unchecked using the current field.

- `value` provides the machine-readable value to be recorded when the user checks the current field.

- `label` provides a human-readable value, shown on the right side of the checkbox.

- `checked` specifies whether the current field is checked or not; by default, the field is not checked.

- `labelWidth` specifies a percent value, used to increase or decrease the width of the label for the current field. By default, the label is quite narrow, and to display long names, it may be unreadable; this property helps to solve this problem.

- `labelWrap` specifies a Boolean value stating whether the label of the current field can be wrapped on several lines; this is false by default, which means that long labels are shown with an ellipsis ("…") at the end.

- `required` specifies whether the current field is mandatory. By default, Sencha Touch adds an asterisk (*) to the field marked as required.

There is a subclass of the `Checkbox` class that has a particular behavior: the `Radio` field type.

```
Ext.define('Chapter5Forms.view.CheckboxSample', {
    extend: 'Ext.form.Panel',
    xtype: 'checkboxsample',
    config: {
        items: [{
            xtype: 'fieldset',
            title: 'Checkboxes',
            instructions: 'Select one or many countries',
            items: [{
                xtype: 'checkboxfield',
                name: 'country', value: 'ar',
                label: 'Argentina', checked: false, labelWidth: '70%'
            }, {
                xtype: 'checkboxfield',
                name: 'country', value: 'fm',
                label: 'Federated States of Micronesia',
                labelWrap: true, labelWidth: '70%', required: false
            }, {
                xtype: 'checkboxfield',
                name: 'country', value: 'ch',
                label: 'Switzerland', checked: true,
                required: true, // ❶
                labelWidth: '70%'
            }, {
                xtype: 'checkboxfield',
                name: 'country', value: 'us',
                label: 'United States', checked: false,
                labelWidth: '70%'
            }]
        }]
    }
});
```

❶ The value `required: true` is responsible for the asterisk shown next to the word "Switzerland" in Figure 5-9.

Checkboxes can be seen in Figure 5-9.

Figure 5-9. Checkboxes (the asterisk highlights a required value)

Radio

The Radio field type is a subclass of the Checkbox class, and it provides a common "radio button" experience to forms; it allows users to select one and only one value from a group of options. The most important thing to remember about creating a Radio button group is to use the same name parameter.

There are two convenient methods provided in this class, helping developers to set and get the values selected in a Radio group: getGroupValue() and setGroupValue(value).

```
Ext.define('Chapter5Forms.view.RadioButtonSample', {
    extend: 'Ext.form.Panel',
    xtype: 'radiobuttonsample',
    config: {
        items: [{
            xtype: 'fieldset',
            title: 'Radio buttons',
            instructions: 'Select only one country',
            items: [{
                xtype: 'radiofield',
                name: 'country',
                value: 'dk',
                label: 'Denmark',
                labelWrap: true
            }, {
                xtype: 'radiofield',
                name: 'country',
                value: 'de',
                label: 'Germany',
                checked: false
```

```
            }, {
                xtype: 'radiofield',
                name: 'country',
                value: 'za',
                label: 'South Africa',
                checked: false
            }, {
                xtype: 'radiofield',
                name: 'country',
                value: 'tw',
                label: 'Taiwan',
                checked: true
            }]
        }]
    }
});
```

Radio buttons can be seen in Figure 5-10.

Figure 5-10. Radio buttons

Slider

This component provides users with an easy-to-use mechanism to enter bounded numeric values in a form. Visually, the field is displayed as a knob that can be dragged left or right, allowing the user to select a value from a continuous set of values.

Several configurations are available:

- `minValue` and `maxValue` provide the lower and upper bounds of the range of values allowed to the user.
- `increment` provides the value used to change the value of the component as the user moves the knob left or right.
- `value` specifies the default value to select when the component is initialized.

There is a special kind of `Slider` called the `Toggle`, described in the next section.

Toggle

This field (somewhat surprisingly, a subclass of `Slider`) is used to enter Boolean values on a form. It supports only two values, `true` and `false` which can be set and retrieved programmatically using the `serValue(value)` and `getValue()` methods provided by the parent `Field` class.

This class can be customized visually using the `minValueCls` and `maxValueCls` properties, to override the visual styles provided by Sencha Touch.

```
Ext.define('Chapter5Forms.view.SliderToggleSample', {
    extend: 'Ext.form.Panel',
    xtype: 'slidertogglesample',
    config: {
        items: [{
            xtype: 'fieldset',
            title: 'Slider and Toggle',
            items: [{
                xtype: 'sliderfield',
                minValue: 10,
                maxValue: 400,
                increment: 10,
                value: 100,
                label: 'Slider',
                name: 'slider'
            }, {
                xtype: 'togglefield',
                label: 'Toggle',
                name: 'toggle',
                value: true
            }]
        }]
    }
});
```

Slider and toggle can be seen in Figure 5-11.

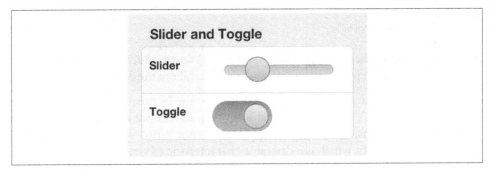

Figure 5-11. Slider and toggle

Using Data with Forms

One of the greatest features of forms is their tight integration with the overall MVC architecture promoted by Sencha Touch. Forms can consume and return instances of Ext.data.Model subclasses, automatically matching the values of individual fields to the properties of data objects.

You can load data into a form using basically two methods:

1. The setValues() method, which takes a literal object with data, whose keys should match the name parameter of the form fields; or:

    ```
    form.setValues({
        name: 'Adrian',
        email: 'adrian@akosma.com',
        password: 'secret'
    });
    ```

2. The setRecord() method, which takes an Ext.data.Model instance as parameter. In this case, the data fields of the model should match the name fields of the form, and Sencha Touch will automatically feed every value on every field:

    ```
    Ext.define('MyApp.model.User', {
        extend: 'Ext.data.Model',
        config: {
            fields: ['name', 'email', 'password']
        }
    });

    var user = Ext.create('MyApp.model.User', {
        name: 'Adrian',
        email: 'adrian@akosma.com',
        password: 'secret'
    });
    ```

```
form.setRecord(ed);
```

As you can imagine, there are matching getValues() and getRecord() methods, which allow the developer to programmatically ask the form about the data stored in the form.

In terms of architectural approach, pay attention to the fact that forms are part of the "view" layer of the MVC architecture; as such, they should not contain business logic or network operations. Separating this code from your forms will allow you to reuse them in other contexts, which is a desirable characteristic of views.

 Please refer to Chapter 6 for a discussion of how to separate the business logic of Sencha Touch applications into dedicated controller classes.

However, for small applications, you can use the submit() method, which basically sends the contents of the form to any URL using a regular POST request.

```
form.submit({
    url: 'url/to/submit/to',
    method: 'POST',
    success: function() {
        alert('form submitted successfully!');
    }
});
```

Conclusion

Forms are a core element of any business application; in Sencha Touch, they include lots of functionality and have a very nice default look and feel, which can be tweaked in lots of different ways. Furthermore, forms integrate beautifully with the MVC architecture of Sencha Touch, providing a very easy abstraction for developers to create data-bound applications in very few steps.

## CHAPTER 6

Controllers

In this chapter we are going to talk about controllers. They are the last piece of the MVC architecture provided by Sencha Touch, and they provide many services that are very useful for software developers creating mobile applications.

Director of the Orchestra

To put it bluntly, the primary objective of controllers is to concentrate power. They provide an interaction layer that sits somewhere between models, stores, and views, and they act as the director of an orchestra, reacting to events, making decisions, and changing the state of the application as needed.

As you saw in Chapter 3, Sencha Touch allows you to provide event handlers for your views, including code that will be executed whenever the user triggers an event on a particular control on the application. These event handlers can be included in the configuration section of any control, using the listeners key.

However handy, this approach leads to unmaintainable and non-reusable code in the long run. It makes the code difficult to learn and debug, not only for new team members, but also for the original team who wrote the code. Finally, it makes reusing code more difficult; what happens if you have several controls whose event handlers are similar, or strictly the same? Should you cut and paste the code?

Controllers provide a concrete answer to this question, including many other interesting features at the same time:

Routing and deep-linking
> Using controllers, you can provide URLs to access different views of your application.

History management
> Sencha Touch uses controllers to support the Back Button available in browsers and in Android devices.

Applications can have as many controllers as required, and even better, many controllers can add event handlers to the same components, each one executing some particular function (in no particular order, though.)

We are going to learn in detail how to use controllers in the following sections.

Creating a Controller

The first task is to create a controller for our application. All Sencha Touch application controllers are instances of the `Ext.app.Controller` class. The following code shows how to create one:

```
Ext.define('Chapter6Controllers.controller.MainController', {
    extend: 'Ext.app.Controller',
    config: {
        refs: {},
        control: {},
        routes: {}
    }
    // Event handlers go here
});
```

Controllers in Sencha Touch are located in the `app/controller` folder, and they have a very simple structure; the `config` section takes only three keys:

- `refs` contains a list of user interface elements, referenced using the `Ext.Component Query` syntax. Each of the elements referenced in this key will automatically be wrapped in a getter function.

- `control` binds one or many entries of the preceding `refs` configuration to the event handlers contained in the controller.

- `routes` provides routing and deep-linking to the application.

 To learn about the `Ext.ComponentQuery` syntax, please refer to Chapter 2.

To make your application load controllers automatically on start-up, remember to add them to the corresponding key in your `Ext.application()` function call:

```
Ext.application({
    name: 'Chapter6Controllers',
    models: // ...
    views: // ...
    controllers: ['MainController'], // ❶
    stores: // ...
    launch: function () {
        // ...
    }
});
```

❶ This will make your controllers available automatically when your application starts.

Let's look at a more complex example to understand how to use controllers.

```
Ext.define('Chapter6Controllers.controller.MainController', {
    extend: 'Ext.app.Controller',
    config: {
        refs: {
            listView: 'indexview > #listView'  // ❶
        },
        control: {
            listView: {
                itemtap: 'listViewItemTap'     // ❷
            }
        }
    },
    listViewItemTap: function(list, index, target, record, e, eOpts) { // ❸
        console.log('list item tap handler: ' + record.get('text'));
    }
});
```

❶ In the refs section of our controller, we use a very simple Ext.Component Query to retrieve a pointer to the list contained inside the component whose xtype is indexview. The name listView is purely arbitrary here, and apart from JavaScript reserved words, you can use any name here (just make sure to reuse it in the file).

❷ Then, in the control section of our configuration, we bind a function to one of the many events exposed by the list component; in this case, we want to listen to the itemtap event, and this will execute a function named listViewItemTap.

❸ Finally, we implement the listViewItemTap function in our controller, using the exact syntax as we would in a normal listeners configuration, and with the same parameters specified in the documentation of the Ext.dataview.List class.

You can reference as many components in your controllers as you want, and you can also reference as many event handlers as required for each of your components. There are not any real rules for the organization of the code in your controllers; your team should decide the best approach on a case-by-case basis, taking into account the functionality of your application and the degree of code reuse that you want to achieve:

```
Ext.define('Chapter6Controllers.controller.MainController', {
    extend: 'Ext.app.Controller',
    config: {
        refs: {
            indexView: 'indexview',
            listView: 'indexview > #listView'
        },
        control: {
            listView: {
                itemsingletap: 'listViewItemTap',
                itemdoubletap: 'listViewDoubleTap'
            },
            indexView: {
                whatever: 'whateverHandler' // ❶
            }
        }
    },
    listViewItemTap: function(list, index, target, record, e, eOpts) {
        console.log('list item single tap handler: ' + record.get('text'));
    },
    listViewDoubleTap: function (list, index, target, record, e, eOpts) {
        console.log('BOOM: list item double tap handler!');
    },
    whateverHandler: function (view) {
        console.log('This is an event handler for a custom event');
    }
});
```

❶   The whatever event is fired by the Chapter6Controllers.view.IndexView class every time an item is selected; please refer to the source code to see how this is done (basically, it involves using the fireEvent() function, just as explained in Chapter 3.)

 Although you can add event handlers in the listeners configuration of your views as well as in one or many controllers, you must pay attention to the fact that they are executed in no particular order; as such, there must be no dependencies among event handlers.

Initialization

As practical as configuration options are, just as with views, sometimes you need to initialize controllers before use. For that, you can use the init() and launch() functions, as shown here:

```
Ext.define('Chapter6Controllers.controller.MainController', {
    extend: 'Ext.app.Controller',
    config: {
        // ...
    },
    init: function () {
        console.log('INIT from MainController');
    },
    launch: function () {
        console.log('LAUNCH from MainController');
    },
    // ...
});
```

When are these functions executed? When a Sencha Touch application starts, there is a very specific sequence of execution followed by all the controllers, the profiles, and the application itself to initialize and prepare for action:

1. All the controllers execute their init() functions first.

2. Then, the current profile ("Tablet", in the following example) executes its own launch() function.

3. After that, the main launch() function (defined in the app.js file) is executed.

4. Finally, the individual launch() functions defined in each controller are executed.

Adding console.log() statements in all of these locations generates the following output:

```
MainController.js:19        INIT from MainController
AnotherController.js:19     INIT from AnotherController
TabletController.js:16      INIT from TabletController
Tablet.js:13                LAUNCH from Tablet profile
app.js:43                   LAUNCH from app.js
MainController.js:22        LAUNCH from MainController
AnotherController.js:22     LAUNCH from AnotherController
TabletController.js:19      LAUNCH from TabletController
```

 Device profiles (such as the Tablet.js file previously mentioned) will be explained in detail in Chapter 10.

Routing and Deep-Linking

Another functionality provided by Sencha Touch controllers is routing and deep-linking. This allows applications to use URLs to refer to individual screens or application states, providing Back button and history support, as well as the possibility of bookmarking or sharing those URLs with other users.

To implement routing, just use a `routes` configuration in your controller:

```
Ext.define('Chapter6Controllers.controller.RoutesController', {
    extend: 'Ext.app.Controller',
    config: {
        refs: {
            splitView: 'akosplitview',
            indexView: 'indexview'
        },
        routes: {
            'checkboxes': 'showCheckboxes',
            'radio': 'showRadioButtons',
            'form': 'showForm',
            'form/:id': 'fillForm'   // ❶
        }
    },
    showCheckboxes: function () {
        var widget = Ext.widget('checkboxsample', {
            title: 'Checkboxes'
        });
        this.showWidget(widget);
    },
    showRadioButtons: function () {
        var widget = Ext.widget('radiobuttonsample', {
            title: 'Radio Buttons'
        });
        this.showWidget(widget);
    },
    showForm: function () {
        var widget = Ext.widget('textfieldsample', {
            title: 'Form'
        });
        this.showWidget(widget);
    },
    fillForm: function (id) {
        var widget = Ext.widget('textfieldsample', {
            title: 'Form'
        });
        widget.down('#sampleTextField').setValue('ID: ' + id); // ❷
        this.showWidget(widget);
    },
    showWidget: function(widget) {
        if (Ext.os.is.Phone) {
            this.getIndexView().push(widget); // ❸
        }
```

```
        else {
            this.getSplitView().displayComponent(widget);
        }
    }
});
```

❶   For each one of the routes that we want to manage, we are going to specify the
     anchor and its associated function. If the anchor includes a parameter, like in
     this case, then the function will receive that parameter at runtime.

❷   The function is executed, and we can retrieve and use that parameter at runtime.

❸   Finally, given that this application uses profiles, it must behave differently
     depending on whether it runs on a smartphone or a tablet.

The result of the previous code is that users can append anchor tags such as #radio,
#checkboxes, or #form/Adrian and the application will behave accordingly, as shown
in Figure 6-1.

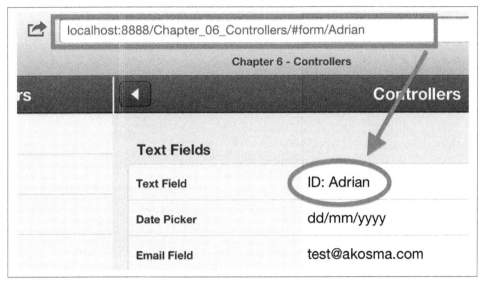

Figure 6-1. Implementing routing with controllers

 When using application profiles, you can avoid having if statements
scattered in your controllers, testing whether your application is running on a phone or a tablet; you should rather use custom controllers
for that! Please refer to Chapter 10 for more information about device
profiles.

Conclusion

This chapter has shown us how to organize the code of our application in a consistent, predictable, and maintainable way. Sencha Touch controllers are a cornerstone in the MVC architecture, providing the required structure and support to centralize all the event handlers of an application in a central location. They also provide support for routing and deep-linking, allowing users to reference screens individually using custom URLs.

## CHAPTER 7

Styling Applications

Creating a good mobile application takes much more than just quality code. The most successful applications have a great personality, conveyed through the proper use of design elements like color, proportion, whitespace, and font choices.

Sencha Touch is no exception to this rule; thankfully, designers can leverage all their current CSS knowledge to provide a strong visual identity to their creations. In this chapter, we are going to learn how Sencha Touch empowers designers to customize the look and feel of their applications.

Using the Default Sencha Styles

The easiest and most straightforward way to style your Sencha Touch application is to use the default CSS files provided by Sencha in the resources/css folder of the framework distribution folder. Just adding the default stylesheets included there will provide a "native" look and feel to your Sencha Touch applications:

```
<!--The default Sencha Touch style-->
<link rel="stylesheet" href="resources/css/sencha-touch.css" />

<!--The default iOS style-->
<link rel="stylesheet" href="resources/css/apple.css" />

<!--The default Android style-->
<link rel="stylesheet" href="resources/css/android.css" />

<!--The default BlackBerry 6 style-->
<link rel="stylesheet" href="resources/css/bb6.css" />
```

You can use these stylesheets in lieu of the default one provided by Sencha in the file sencha-touch.css on the same folder. You can see the different look and feel of the same application, using these default stylesheets, in Figure 7-1: from left to right, the default Sencha Touch style, the iOS style, the Android style, and the BlackBerry 6 style.

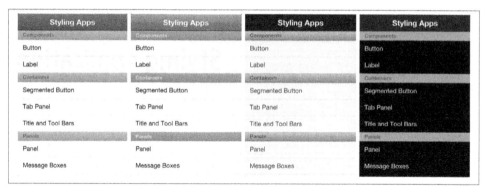

Figure 7-1. Comparison of the default stylesheets

Introduction to Sass

As useful and practical as the standard stylesheets are, most designers will prefer crafting a more personalized look and feel for their applications. Thankfully, Sencha Touch has an incredibly powerful theming subsystem built on top of Sass (*http://sass-lang.com/*), or "Syntactically Awesome Stylesheets." Sass is a superset of CSS, which adds features like nesting, variables, mixins, and inheritance to standard CSS.

Sass stylesheets can be compiled into standard CSS using Compass (*http://compass-style.org/*), an authoring tool based on Ruby.

 In order to use Sass and Compass, please make sure that your developer environment includes a working Ruby installation:

- OS X ships with a working Ruby installation that can be used out of the box.
- Windows users need to download and install Ruby from rubyinstaller.org (*http://rubyinstaller.org/*).
- Finally, Linux users can install Ruby using the package manager included with their favorite distribution.

To install Compass, just use the standard RubyGems command: `gem install compass`.

Sass files have the `.scss` extension, which basically stands for "Sassy CSS" or "SCSS" for short. Also, it is worth pointing out that every CSS file is a valid SCSS file.

Sass allows developers to create and maintain more complex stylesheets than with standard CSS, including the following features:

- Variables
- Nesting
- Inheritance
- Functions, including very useful color manipulations
- Mixins

The following sections provide a quick introduction to each one of these features.

Variables

Sass allows developers to define variables, providing reuse and readability to long style-sheets. Variables are simply declared using the $ sign in front of the name, and can be used throughout the stylesheet afterward:

```
/* ---------- Sass ---------- */

$blue: #9dbed3;
$margin: 5px;

#p {
    background-color: $blue;
    margin-top: $margin
}


/* ---------- Generated CSS ---------- */

#p {
    background-color: #9dbed3;
    margin-top: 10px;
}
```

Variable expressions can also contain arithmetic calculations involving different units, liberating the developer from performing complex calculations:

```
/* ---------- Sass ---------- */

$height: 920px;

div.instructions {
    width: 2in + 7pt;
    height: $height / 2;
}


/* ---------- Generated CSS ---------- */

div.instructions {
    width: 2.09722in;
```

```
        height: 460px;
    }
```

Nesting

Nesting directives allows developers to avoid repeating themselves, which is all too common in standard CSS:

```
/* ---------- Sass ---------- */

body {
    font: {
        family: Times;
        weight: bold;
        size: 1em;
    }
}

#div {
    background-color: gray;

    .emphasize {
        text-decoration: underline;
    }
}


/* ---------- Generated CSS ---------- */

body {
    font-family: Times;
    font-weight: bold;
    font-size: 1em;
}

#div {
    background-color: gray;
}

#div .emphasize {
    text-decoration: underline;
}
```

Inheritance

Just like in many programming languages, and somewhat similarly to nesting, Sass uses inheritance to make a directive automatically replicate CSS instructions elsewhere in the final stylesheet:

```
/* ---------- Sass ---------- */
```

```scss
.alert {
    font-size: 0.9em;
    background-color: gray;
}

.alert.important {
    font-weight: bold;
}

.redalert {
    @extend .alert;
    background-color: red;
}


/* ---------- Generated CSS ---------- */

.alert, .redalert {
    font-size: 0.9em;
    background-color: yellow;
}

.alert.important, .redalert.important {
    font-weight: bold;
}

.redalert {
    background-color: red;
}
```

Functions

Sass also provides a large set of pre-built functions (*http://sass-lang.com/docs/yardoc/ Sass/Script/Functions.html*), ready to be used, working on the following data types:

- Colors
- Booleans
- Strings
- Numbers
- Lists

Here are some useful functions provided by Sass:

- quote( ) and unquote( ), for strings
- length( ) and nth( ), for lists
- min( ), max( ), abs( ), ceil( ), and floor( ) for numbers

- Finally, `type-of()`, `unit()`, and `if()`, which are more generic functions

Color manipulation

Among its built-in functions, Sass has an impressive array of color manipulation ones, all built on top of the `Color` (*http://sass-lang.com/docs/yardoc/Sass/Script/Color.html*) type. Color objects in Sass have the following methods and properties (among others):

- `alpha`
- `red`, `green`, and `blue`
- `hue`, `saturation`, and `lightness`

Color objects can be passed as parameters, converted into other representations, and combined with other colors.

```
/* Create a custom color */
$red: 18;
$green: 152;
$blue: 227;
$alpha: 0.7;
$blue: rgba($red, $green, $blue, $alpha);

/* Manipulate the color */
$list-color: complement(darken($blue, 20%));
```

Just like `complement` and `darken`, other useful color manipulation functions are the following:

- `darken()` and `lighten()`
- `saturate()` and `desaturate()`
- `complement()` and `invert()`
- `opacify()` and `transparentize()`
- `ie-hex-str($color)`, which returns a color definition compatible with IE filters

Mixins

Mixins provide a very simple way to encapsulate and reuse chunks of CSS code throughout your stylesheet, without having to repeat them everywhere. They are declared using the `@mixin` keyword, they can take any number and type of variables and are used with the `@include` keyword:

```
/* ---------- Sass ---------- */

@mixin some-special-style($color, $font-size) {
```

```
    font: {
        family: serif;
        size: $font-size;
    }
    color: $color;
}

div.special {
    @include some-special-style(red, 45pt);
    margin: 1em;
}

div.notsospecial {
    @include some-special-style(green, 3em);
    margin: 1em;
    padding: 10px;
    background-color: yellow;
}


/* ---------- Generated CSS ---------- */

div.special {
    font-family: serif;
    font-size: 45pt;
    color: red;
    margin: 1em;
}

div.notsospecial {
    font-family: serif;
    font-size: 3em;
    color: green;
    margin: 1em;
    padding: 10px;
    background-color: yellow;
}
```

Using Sass in Sencha Touch

To start using Sass with Sencha Touch, we are going to style one of the applications we created in the previous chapters. To do that, the first thing we need to do is to create a resources folder in the project and then copy the following two files, usually located in the /resources/sass folder of the Sencha Touch distribution:

- config.rb
- sencha-touch.scss

After this is done, the config.rb file has to be modified, so that it automatically includes the Sencha Touch libraries. This usually involves using the File.join() Ruby method call, and setting up the proper path to the Sencha Touch distribution folder:

```
# Get the directory that this configuration file exists in
dir = File.dirname(__FILE__)

# Load the sencha-touch framework automatically.
load File.join(dir, '..', '..', '_libs', 'sencha', 'resources', 'themes')

# Compass configurations
sass_path    = dir
css_path     = File.join(dir, "..", "css")
environment  = :production

# Remember to set 'output_style = :compressed' before going on
# production!
#
# output_style = :compressed
output_style = :expanded
```

On the other hand, the default sencha-touch.scss file has the following structure:

```
@import 'sencha-touch/default/all';

@include sencha-panel;
@include sencha-buttons;
@include sencha-sheet;
@include sencha-picker;
@include sencha-tabs;
@include sencha-toolbar;
@include sencha-toolbar-forms;
@include sencha-indexbar;
@include sencha-list;
@include sencha-list-paging;
@include sencha-list-pullrefresh;
@include sencha-layout;
@include sencha-carousel;
@include sencha-form;
@include sencha-msgbox;
@include sencha-loading-spinner;
```

In the preceding snippet, it is important to make the following distinctions:

- @import is used to dynamically import SCSS statements in an external file. This directive is used by the Sass compiler when the final CSS file is generated.

- On the other hand, @include is used to import Sass "mixins," which are reusable blocks of Sass commands that might include parameters.

Generating CSS with Compass

To generate the final CSS from the Sass files, we are going to use the Compass tool. Compass watches a certain folder in the file system waiting for changes and triggers the compilation of the Sass sources automatically. For this, we need to first launch the tool with the following command:

```
$ compass watch [dirname]
```

 tmux (*http://tmux.sourceforge.net/*) is particularly helpful in this situation, since it is very convenient to leave a tmux window or pane with Compass running in it as the developer works with the CSS files.

However, if you do not want to use Compass, and you are using LiveReload (*http://livereload.com*), you can configure it to automatically generate CSS files from your Sass source files.

On the other hand, if you want to use Compass but would rather not use a command line tool for that, then you can use Compass.app (*http://compass.handlino.com/*), a cross-platform (Linux, Windows, and OS X) tool.

The output of the execution of this command looks like this:

```
$ compass watch .

Dear developers making use of FSSM in your projects,
FSSM is essentially dead at this point. Further development will
be taking place in the new shared guard/listen project. Please
let us know if you need help transitioning! ^_^b
- Travis Tilley

>>> Compass is polling for changes. Press Ctrl-C to Stop.
>>> Change detected at 08:02:16 to: sencha-touch.scss
overwrite ./../css/sencha-touch.css
>>> Change detected at 08:02:35 to: sencha-touch.scss
overwrite ./../css/sencha-touch.css
>>> Change detected at 10:20:55 to: sencha-touch.scss
error sencha-touch.scss (Line 21: Invalid CSS after "$list-color: ":
expected expression (e.g. 1px, bold), was ";")
Sass::SyntaxError on line ["21"] of
sass/sencha-touch.scss: Invalid CSS after
"$list-color: ": expected expression (e.g. 1px, bold), was ";"
Run with --trace to see the full backtrace
>>> Change detected at 10:21:15 to: sencha-touch.scss
overwrite ./../css/sencha-touch.css
>>> Change detected at 10:21:22 to: sencha-touch.scss
identical ./../css/sencha-touch.css
>>> Change detected at 10:34:57 to: sencha-touch.scss
overwrite ./../css/sencha-touch.css
```

As explained by the tool, you can press the Ctrl+C key combination at any time to stop the watch and rebuild the process. Also, as previously shown, the compiler informs the developer in case of errors in the source Sass file.

Using Sencha Cmd

Applications generated with Sencha Cmd include a resources/sass folder by default, which is taken into account automatically (that is, compiled and minified) every time an application is packaged or built using the command line tools. This is explained in detail in Chapter 10.

Sencha Touch Sass Parameters

Sencha Touch uses Sass extensively, and there are many global variables that can be "tweaked" and fine-tuned to modify the look and feel of your application. Among those variables, the most important are the following:

- $base-color, which specifies the original color, used throughout the Sass system to style the whole application. Many styles use this variable, modifying it through Sass functions, to provide a unified and elegant look to your application.

- $base-gradient takes the values bevel, glossy, recessed, and matte (the latter one being the default value). This gradient is used in title bars and list section headers.

- $active-color is the color used by pickers, action buttons, and selected rows in lists.

- $font-family specifies the base font to be used in the application.

- $global-row-height determines the size of list rows (usually 46 pixels by default).

- $include-border-radius is a Boolean value that specifies whether buttons and other elements should display rounded corners or not.

- $include-default-icons specifies whether the default icons included in Sencha Touch (as explained in Chapter 3) have to be included or not. If you do not use tab bars or toolbars in your application, then setting this value to false will save you a great amount of space and bandwidth, because these icons are included as base-64 encoded images in the CSS file.

- $neutral-color is the color used by toolbars and tab bars for the ui style.

- $page-bg-color is the background color used by components set to fullscreen.

In addition to these global Sass variables, each UI component in Sencha Touch exposes a certain number of variables, and all of them are explained in the documentation system, as shown in Figure 7-2.

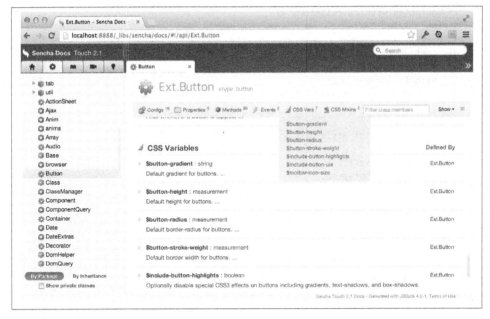

Figure 7-2. Documentation page for styles

After customization, our application features (at least in iOS 6, where the font named "AvenirNextCondensed-DemiBold" is available) a really customized look, as shown in Figure 7-3, using the following Sass file:

```
/* Here we override global variables as required by our design */

/* Custom color */
$red: 18;
$green: 152;
$blue: 227;
$alpha: 0.7;
$blue: rgba($red, $green, $blue, $alpha);

/* Base parameters */
$base-color: $blue;
$font-family: AvenirNextCondensed-DemiBold, sans;
$include-border-radius: false;
$base-gradient: recessed; /* bevel, glossy, recessed, matte (default) */

/* Buttons */
$button-height: 2em;
$include-button-uis: false;

/* Lists */
$list-color: complement(darken($blue, 20%));
$list-zebrastripe: true;
```

```
/* Variables with calculations */
$height: 920px;

div.instructions {
    width: 2in + 7pt;
    height: $height / 2;
}

/* Mixins */
@mixin some-special-style($color, $font-size) {
    font: {
        family: serif;
        size: $font-size;
    }
    color: $color;
}

div.special {
    @include some-special-style(red, 45pt);
    margin: 1em;
}

div.notsospecial {
    @include some-special-style(green, 3em);
    margin: 1em;
    padding: 10px;
    background-color: yellow;
}


@import 'sencha-touch/default/all';

@include sencha-panel;
@include sencha-buttons;
@include sencha-sheet;
@include sencha-picker;
@include sencha-tabs;
@include sencha-toolbar;
@include sencha-indexbar;
@include sencha-list;
@include sencha-layout;
@include sencha-msgbox;
@include sencha-loading-spinner;
@include sencha-draw;

/*
You should remove elements that are not used, to make the resulting CSS
smaller and faster to download:

@include sencha-toolbar-forms;
@include sencha-carousel;
```

```
@include sencha-list-paging;
@include sencha-list-pullrefresh;
@include sencha-form;
@include sencha-charts;
*/
```

Remove unused styles!
To make the final CSS file smaller, you can comment out (or remove altogether) one or many of the @include statements at the end of the Sass file; this way, your production CSS file will contain only the styles and definitions that are actually required.

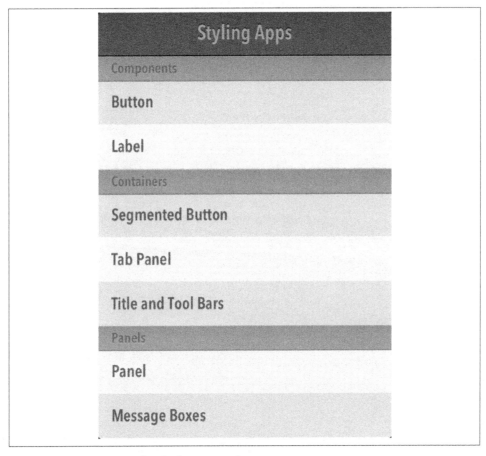

Figure 7-3. A customized style for our application

Conclusion

Sencha Touch uses Sass extensively, allowing designers to customize the look and feel of their applications completely. Not only that, but the API documentation system includes all the references required to know the name of the variables to be overridden throughout the system.

Even better, Sencha Touch includes pre-cooked CSS files reproducing the styles of iOS, Android, and BlackBerry applications, making it very easy to integrate Sencha Touch applications in these environments.

## CHAPTER 8

Debugging, Testing, and Documenting

More than with any other programming language, the dynamic nature of JavaScript makes it fundamental to have the proper tools in order to increase the quality of our applications. This chapter will provide an introduction to some important tools used for debugging, testing, and documenting Sencha Touch applications.

Of course, "testing" is a rather large concept, and it would be foolish to pretend that this chapter will give you a complete overview of testing Sencha Touch apps. However, these simple techniques will allow you and your team to increase your quality, helping you ship code on schedule.

Debugging

Debugging your application is certainly an art. Thankfully, JavaScript developers do not need to rely on the good old alert() debugging technique anymore. In this section, we are going to learn about more modern and effective ways to debug your application:

- WebKit Web Inspector
- Remote Debugging (for iOS 6 and OS X Mountain Lion)
- Adobe Edge Inspect (formerly "Adobe Shadow" and "weinre")

WebKit Web Inspector

The first tool that will be used to debug mobile web applications is the Web Inspector that ships natively with WebKit-based browsers. It is a very powerful tool, originally inspired by the famous Firebug plug-in for Firefox by Joe Hewitt; these days, the WebKit Web Inspector, Opera DragonFly, or the Internet Explorer Developer Tools all allow you to perform the following functions:

- Inspect the HTML structure of the current web page, including all elements that are generated dynamically (this is especially handy in the case of Sencha Touch, which generates HTML elements on the fly).

- Set breakpoints in your JavaScript code, to debug your code and to verify that everything works as expected.

- Explore the different HTML5 storage options of your browser, including databases, cookies, or the `localStorage`.

- Modify the CSS of your page dynamically, changing properties and seeing them "live" on your page, which is a huge help for designers and developers alike.

 In the case of Sencha Touch, the requirement of using WebKit-based mobile browsers restricts our choice of development tools a bit, to just Apple Safari or Google Chrome. At least at the time of this writing, you cannot use Firebug on Firefox or other browsers to inspect your applications.

Enable the WebKit Inspector

To enable the WebKit Inspector in Google Chrome or Apple Safari, follow these steps:

- In Google Chrome, in the View menu, select the Developer entry, and click Developer Tools.

- In Apple Safari, open the Preferences panel, and in the Advanced tab, check the "Show Develop menu in menu bar" option, as shown in Figure 8-1.

 Latest versions of Chrome and Safari
At the time of this writing, the latest version of Google Chrome was 23, and the latest version of Apple Safari for OS X Mountain Lion was 6.0.2.

 Different UIs
Please pay attention to the fact that the user experience of the web inspector in Safari 6 has been extensively modified from the version shipped in Chrome.

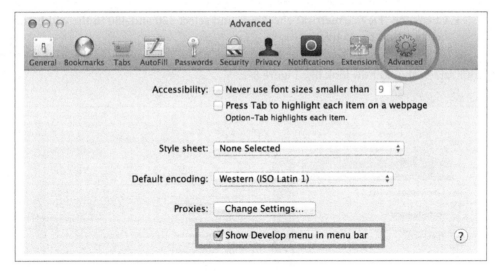

Figure 8-1. Safari Preferences panel

Setup for mobile development

The following setup is recommended for working with the WebKit Web Inspector on Chrome:

1. Open Chrome and navigate to the URL of your Sencha Touch application in the development web server.

2. Right-click the application and select Inspect Element; this will open the WebKit inspector, which by default appears in the lower section of the screen.

3. Open the inspector settings, clicking on the Settings button on the lower-right corner of the inspector (outlined in Figure 8-2.)

4. In the General tab of the settings screen (shown in Figure 8-3) select the following options:

   • "Dock to right," to make the inspector appear on the right side of the Chrome window, instead of on the bottom.

   • "Disable cache," to avoid having bad surprises because of cached files when re-loading source code files.

5. In the Overrides tab, select the following options (as shown in Figure 8-4):

   • Check the User Agent checkbox and select "iPhone - iOS 5" in the drop-down menu.

- Check the "Device metrics" checkbox, and select 320 and 480 in the width and height fields, respectively.

Your screen should now look like Figure 8-2.

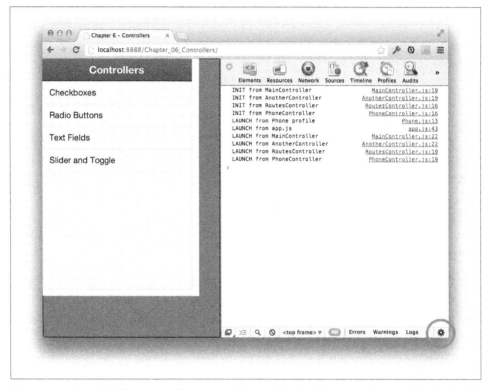

Figure 8-2. Google Chrome WebKit setup for mobile development (settings highlighted)

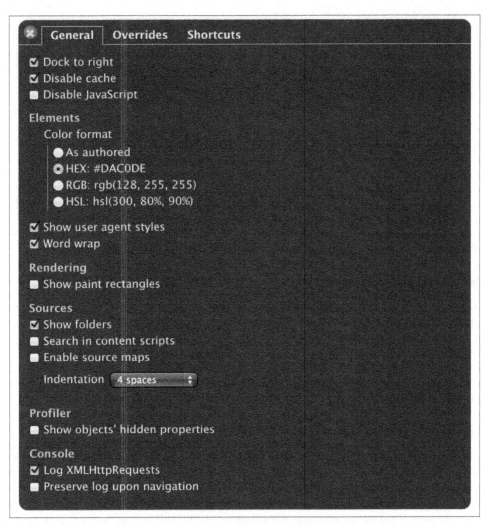

Figure 8-3. General tab of the Google Chrome WebKit inspector settings

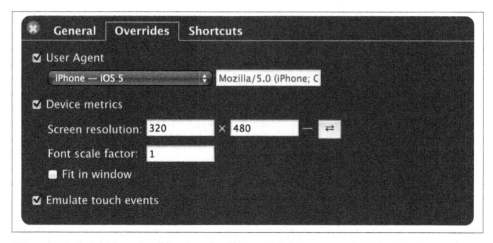

Figure 8-4. Overrides tab of the Google Chrome WebKit inspector settings

Inspect the HTML of your app

Using the web inspector, you can see the complete structure of your page, including all the nested elements, and including those that are created during runtime. This is particularly useful when debugging the HTML code created by frameworks like Sencha Touch.

Figure 8-5 shows how the WebKit Inspector highlights the UI of the application as the user hovers over the corresponding areas of the HTML code.

Log messages in the console

Using the console, you can inspect the internal state of your application without having to use the old `alert()` way of doing things. There are two different instructions that you can use to output text to the console:

- `console.log(message)`, where `message` is a string, will output that text to the console. If the object is not a string, then the result of the `toString()` method will be displayed.

- `console.dir(object)` will display the complete structure of an object in the console, allowing you to see its internal tree structure.

 Some inspectors perform the same task when invoking `console.log()` and `console.dir()`; as always, there might be differences across browsers and even among versions of the same browser. However, both methods are supported these days.

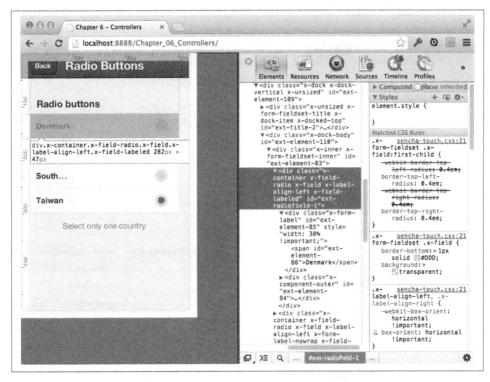

Figure 8-5. Inspecting the HTML

Figure 8-6 shows many messages printed in the console of the WebKit Inspector (all generated by the sample application from Chapter 6).

Set breakpoints

Finally, the web inspector allows you to set breakpoints in your JavaScript code, which helps developers to execute their programs instruction by instruction, to see the values of the variables in the current stack frames, and to step in and out from functions, lambdas, and methods.

Figure 8-6. Using breakpoints

Remote Debugging

Starting with iOS 6 and Safari 6, included in OS X 10.8 Mountain Lion, developers can use new remote debugging capabilities, allowing them to inspect the internal workings of their application in real time, whether it is running on the iOS Simulator or in an iOS device connected through a USB cable. This method works for applications using Mobile Safari, standalone browser applications (those "saved on home screen" among other applications), and also applications using UIWebView (such as applications packaged using Sencha Cmd or PhoneGap (*http://phonegap.com*)).

 This section applies only to developers and devices using iOS 6 or higher, and OS X 10.8 Mountain Lion or higher.

To take advantage of remote debugging on iOS and OS X, follow these steps:

1. Load your Sencha Touch application, either on the iOS Simulator or on your iOS device of choice.

If using an iOS device, remember to plus its USB cable to your Mac.

2. In Safari, select the Developer menu and select either the iPhone Simulator or the menu with the name of your iOS device.

3. In the submenu, select the application you wish to debug. As you are selecting it, the application is highlighted to help the developer choose the correct one.

This operation will open a standalone WebKit Inspector window, like the one shown in Figure 8-7. Using this window, you can perform the typical debugging operations previously described, with the added benefit of running your application in an environment that closely resembles that of normal production.

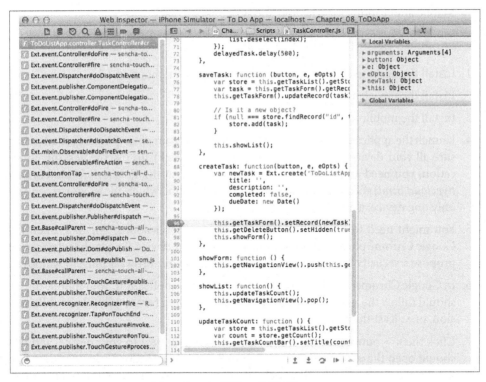

Figure 8-7. Using remote debugging in iOS and OS X

Adobe Edge Inspect

As useful as remote debugging is, it works only with iOS 6 and OS X Mountain Lion, and you might want to inspect the state of your application as it runs in an Android device, or to use Windows to perform the debugging session; to help you with that, the Adobe Edge Inspect (*http://html.adobe.com/edge/inspect/*) tool is there.

Adobe Edge Inspect (formerly known as "Adobe Shadow") is based on a project originally created by the PhoneGap team, called weinre (*http://phonegap.github.com/weinre/*) (this name stands for Web Inspector Remote). Adobe acquired weinre during the merge of PhoneGap and has packaged it in a way that makes it very easy to use.

Adobe Edge Inspect consists of the following elements:

- Desktop applications for Mac and Windows
- A Google Chrome plug-in
- Mobile applications for Android and iOS

To use Adobe Edge Inspect, follow these steps:

1. Install the desktop application on the system of your choice.
2. Install the Google Chrome plug-in.
3. Install the mobile application in your device.
4. Launch the applications in both your computer and your smartphone or iPad (make sure all your devices are in the same wireless network). To use the desktop application, you need an Adobe Creative Cloud (*http://www.adobe.com/products/creativecloud.html*) account, but you can use a free account, which allows you to connect only one device at a time.
5. You might need to pair the mobile and desktop applications. For that, open the Google Chrome plug-in and select the name of your device. The mobile device will propose a security code that you should type into your browser plug-in window.
6. In Google Chrome, navigate to the URL of your web application. Your mobile device should follow the navigation automatically, displaying (eventually) the mobile version, or at least the same page.
7. Click the < > button on the Google Chrome plug-in next to your device, and this should open the window shown in Figure 8-8. In that window, select the device in the Remote tab and use the web inspector window as you normally would. Figure 8-9 shows the result of dynamically invoking Ext.Msg.alert() on the device, which triggers a dialog to appear on the device.

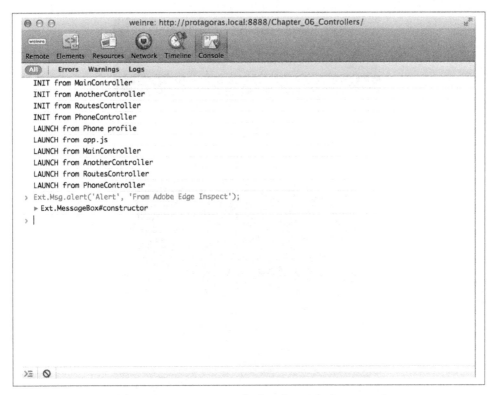

Figure 8-8. Adobe Edge Inspect session, including live DOM manipulation

This works on iOS and Android devices over the local network. At the moment of this writing, Adobe Edge Inspect still does not allow for setting breakpoints and for executing JavaScript code step by step, but hopefully this functionality will be included soon. Also, bear in mind that with a free Adobe Creative Cloud account, you can connect only one device at a time.

Figure 8-9. Adobe Edge Inspect session on an iOS device

Testing

This section will introduce one open source and one commercial testing framework that you can use to test your Sencha Touch applications:

- Jasmine (*https://github.com/pivotal/jasmine*)
- Siesta (*http://www.bryntum.com/products/siesta/*)

The sample To Do List application, shown in Figure 8-10, demonstrates each of these frameworks. This application is a very simple Sencha Touch MVC application, including two views, a model, a store, and a controller.

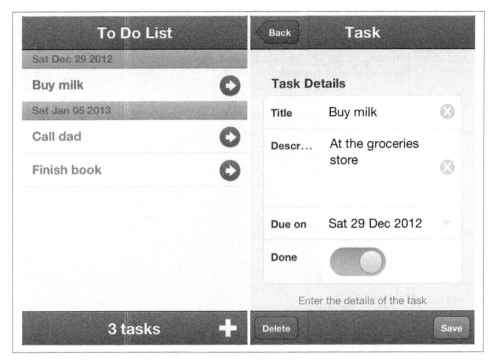

Figure 8-10. To Do List sample application

Jasmine

Test-driven development (TDD) has probably been one of the major breakthroughs of the past 15 years. Nearly every programming language has at least one unit testing library, but lately the fashion has gone to the new field of behavior-driven development (BDD), in which the suite of tests will "describe" the actions taken by the piece of software being considered, evaluating the output against some predetermined values.

The idea behind BDD is not only to test the possible outcomes of a piece of software, but also to provide a living documentation that can be used by other developers, or even by customers, to verify the correct mechanisms of their software.

Jasmine is a JavaScript BDD library that has two special characteristics to it: First, it does not require the DOM to work; this means that it is implemented using core JavaScript objects and APIs, and that Jasmine tests can run outside the browser. The second interesting fact is that Jasmine does not depend on other libraries; this means that it's extremely simple to install and use.

The latest available version of Jasmine at the time of this writing is 1.3.1. You can also try Jasmine without installing it on your machine just by browsing to the Try Jasmine (*http://tryjasmine.com/*) site, created by the developers of Jasmine.

As a very simple example, let's use Jasmine to test the `ToDoListApp.model.Task` class used by the To Do List application:

```
Ext.define('ToDoListApp.model.Task', {
    extend: 'Ext.data.Model',
    config: {
        identifier: 'uuid',
        fields: [{
            name: 'id',
            type: 'int'
        }, {
            name: 'completed',
            type: 'boolean'
        }, {
            name: 'dueDate',
            type: 'date'
        }, {
            name: 'title',
            type: 'string',
            defaultValue: ''
        }, {
            name: 'description',
            type: 'string'
        }],
        idProperty: 'id'
    }
});
```

To do that, we have first to download the latest Jasmine library (*https://github.com/pivotal/jasmine/tags*) from Github. Inside the Jasmine distribution there is a `lib/jasmine-core/example` folder, containing a file named `SpecRunner.html`. We are going to modify that file and include our own classes:

```
<!DOCTYPE HTML PUBLIC "-//W3C//DTD HTML 4.01 Transitional//EN"
    "http://www.w3.org/TR/html4/loose.dtd">
<html>
<head>
    <title>Jasmine Spec Runner</title>

    <link rel="shortcut icon" type="image/png" href="lib/jasmine_favicon.png">
    <link rel="stylesheet" type="text/css" href="lib/jasmine.css">

    <script type="text/javascript" src="lib/jasmine.js"></script>
    <script type="text/javascript" src="lib/jasmine-html.js"></script>
```

```
<!--include a console runner here-->
<script type="text/javascript" src="lib/console-runner.js"></script>

<!-- include source files here... -->
<script src="/_libs/sencha/sencha-touch-all-debug.js"></script> ❶

<!-- test launcher -->
<script type="text/javascript" src="src/AppTest.js"></script> ❷

<!-- include spec files here... -->
<script type="text/javascript" src="src/TaskSpec.js"></script> ❸

<script type="text/javascript">
  (function() {
    var jasmineEnv = jasmine.getEnv();
    jasmineEnv.updateInterval = 1000;

    var htmlReporter = new jasmine.HtmlReporter();

    jasmineEnv.addReporter(htmlReporter);

    window.consoleReporter = new jasmine.ConsoleReporter();
    jasmineEnv.addReporter(consoleReporter);

    jasmineEnv.specFilter = function(spec) {
      return htmlReporter.specFilter(spec);
    };

    var currentWindowOnload = window.onload;

    window.onload = function() {
      if (currentWindowOnload) {
        currentWindowOnload();
      }
      execJasmine();
    };

    function execJasmine() {
      jasmineEnv.execute();
    }

  })();
</script>

</head>

<body>
</body>
</html>
```

❶   Here we load the Sencha Touch library files.

❷   This file contains the definition of the application we want to test.

❸   This file contains the spec files that describe the tests.

We also need to create a simpler version of our app.js file in order to bootstrap and load the required files during the testfootnote. This bootstrap file has been adapted from the one used in the documentation of Ext JS 4.1 (*http://docs.sencha.com/ext-js/4-1/#!/ guide/testing*):

```
Ext.require('Ext.app.Application');

Ext.Loader.setConfig({
    paths: {
        'ToDoListApp': '../Chapter_08_ToDoApp/app'
    }
});

var Application = null;

Ext.onReady(function() {
    Application = Ext.create('Ext.app.Application', {
        name: 'ToDoListApp',
        models: [ 'Task' ],

        launch: function() {
            //include the tests in the test.html head
            jasmine.getEnv().addReporter(new jasmine.TrivialReporter());
            jasmine.getEnv().execute();
        }
    });
});
```

A suite of tests written with a BDD library is usually called a "spec." The spec file looks like a complete description of the behavior and structure of the class being tested. Jasmine provides functions named describe, grouping several calls to a function called it.

```
describe ("Task", function() {
    var task = null;

    beforeEach (function() {
        task = Ext.create('ToDoListApp.model.Task');
    });

    describe ("when a new one is created", function () {
        it ("should have an empty description", function () {
            expect(task.get('description')).toBeNull();
        });

        it ("should have an empty name", function () {
            expect(task.get('title')).toEqual('');
        });
```

```
        it ("should not be completed", function () {
            expect(task.get('completed')).toBeFalsy();
        });
    });

    describe ("when one is modified", function () {
        it ("should have the description passed as parameter", function () {
            var newDescription = "Whatever";
            task.set('description', newDescription);
            expect(task.get('description')).toEqual(newDescription);
        });

        it ("should have the specified date", function () {
            var newDate = new Date();
            task.set('duedate', newDate);
            expect(task.get('duedate')).toEqual(newDate);
        });

        it ("should have the specified completed status", function () {
            task.set('completed', true);
            expect(task.get('completed')).toBeTruthy();
        });

        it ("should have the name specified as parameter", function () {
            var newName = "new name";
            task.set('title', newName);
            expect(task.get('title')).toEqual(newName);
        });
    });

    describe ("when one is reset", function () {
        it ("should not be marked as done", function () {
            task.set('completed', false);
            expect(task.get('completed')).toBeFalsy();
        });
    });
});
```

Reloading the SpecRunner.html file on the browser provides the following output, showing that all the tests have passed, and outputting the texts passed as parameters of the describe and it functions. The result is shown in Figure 8-11.

Finally, we can also run the tests from the command line, thanks to the PhantomJS open-source library (*http://phantomjs.org/*), itself powered by the WebKit engine.

 You can install PhantomJS in OS X using Homebrew (*http://mxcl.github.com/homebrew/*).

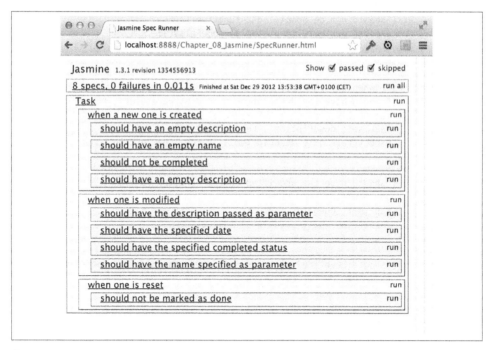

Figure 8-11. Jasmine output

If your development environment already contains PhantomJS, and assuming that you can access the code samples at http://localhost, then you can type the following command line in the Chapter_08_Jasmine folder of the source code for this book:

```
$  phantomjs  lib/run_jasmine_test.coffee  http://localhost/Chapter_08_Jasmine/
SpecRunner.html
Starting...
Starting...
Task when a new one is created: 3 of 3 passed.
Task when one is modified: 4 of 4 passed.
Task when one is reset: 1 of 1 passed.

Finished
----------------
8 specs, 0 failures in 0.006s.

ConsoleReporter finished
```

This technique can be leveraged to have nightly automatic test runs for your projects and is based in Joshua Carver's Jasmine runner for Phantom.js (*https://github.com/ jcarver989/phantom-jasmine*), freely available on Github.

Siesta

Another tool that we are going to introduce in this chapter is Siesta (*http://bryntum.com/products/siesta/*), a commercial JavaScript testing framework that targets many frameworks, such as jQuery, Dojo, and Prototype, and of course also Ext JS and very recently Sencha Touch.

Using Siesta, developers can automate integration testing tasks on their applications, simulating touches and navigation throughout their Sencha Touch apps. They can be used to test not only individual components, but also whole applications, including the interaction between screens and the navigation.

This is simplified because Siesta is aware of many exclusive features of both Ext JS and Sencha Touch, like the `Ext.ComponentQuery` syntax, providing a higher level of abstraction than other testing frameworks. Not only that, but Siesta is also able to work in asynchronous modes, waiting for classes to be loaded dynamically (using the `requireOk()` function). It is also aware of the MVC structure of Sencha Touch apps, including stores and models.

Siesta is a product of Bryntum (*http://bryntum.com/*), a company in Helsingborg, Sweden, started by Mats Bryntse (*https://twitter.com/bryntum*). Siesta is available in two versions: **Lite**, which is provided free of charge, and **Standard**, providing enterprise features like premium support, cross page testing, and Selenium (*http://seleniumhq.org/*) integration.

Siesta Standard unit test suites can also be executed on the command line, using PhantomJS (*http://phantomjs.org/*) or Node.js (*http://nodejs.org/*). This simplifies the integration of tests in larger, continuous integration chains. It can also be used to perform "black box" testing, by using the `hostPageUrl` option.

We are going to show how to create a simple testing suite for our To Do List application. The first thing we need to do is to create a bootstrap HTML and JavaScript file that will be used to display the tests as they are executed.

```
<!DOCTYPE html>
<html>
    <head>
        <!-- Sencha Touch library CSS-->
        <link rel="stylesheet"
        href="../../_libs/sencha/resources/css/sencha-touch.css">
        <title>Testing with Siesta</title>

        <!-- Siesta CSS -->
        <link rel="stylesheet"
        href="siesta-1.1.0-preview/resources/css/siesta-touch-all.css">
    </head>
    <body>
        <div id="splashLoader">
```

```
            <div id="loading">
                <span class="loadTxt">Loading...</span>
                <div class="x-loading-spinner"><span class="x-loading-top">
                    </span><span class="x-loading-right"></span><span class="x-
loading-bottom">
                    </span><span class="x-loading-left"></span></div>
                </div>
            </div>

            <!-- Sencha Touch library -->
            <script src="../../_libs/sencha/sencha-touch-all-debug.js"></script>

            <!-- Siesta application -->
            <script src="siesta-1.1.0-preview/siesta-touch-all.js"></script>

            <!-- The test harness -->
            <script src="index.js"></script>
        </body>
    </html>
```

This HTML file references the Sencha Touch 2 and the Siesta libraries, each composed of a JavaScript and a CSS file.

The next step is to create a JavaScript file that will be used to describe the suite of tests to be executed:

```
var Harness = Siesta.Harness.Browser.SenchaTouch;

Harness.configure({
    title         : 'Testing the To Do List Application',
    transparentEx : false,
    loaderPath    : { 'ToDoListApp' : '/Sencha%20Touch/todoapp/app' }
});

Harness.start(
    {
        group : 'To Do List',

        // Load these files for each ST 2.0 test
        preload : [
            "/_libs/sencha/sencha-touch-all-debug.js",
            "/_libs/sencha/resources/css/sencha-touch.css"
        ],
        items : [
            'tests/sanity.js',
            'tests/model.js',
            'tests/createTask.js'
        ]
    }
);
```

Siesta requires various pieces of JavaScript code to define tests:

1. A "test harness," which will reference individual tests.

2. One or more individual test files, each testing an individual section of the application. Each test file runs in a completely isolated scope from other test files, separating different test scenarios from one another.

The configuration of the harness in the preceding script uses the loaderPath key, which is required by Siesta when dealing with MVC applications that use the Sencha Loader mechanism. We are providing, as a parameter, the location of the Sencha Application being tested.

Figure 8-12 shows the screen displayed when the user navigates to the testing harness from within the Mobile Safari browser in an iOS device.

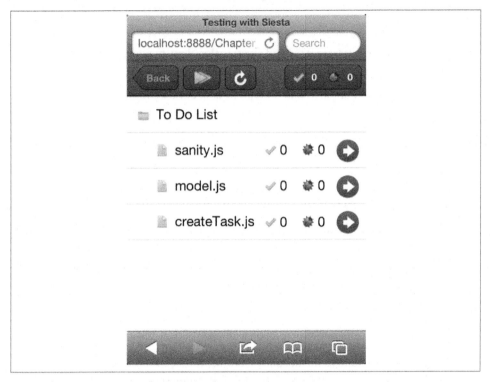

Figure 8-12. Siesta before executing the tests

Each individual testing file targets a particular aspect of the application being tested; for example, tests/model.js tests the ToDoListApp.model.Task class:

```
StartTest(function(t) {
    t.diag("Testing Task model");
```

```
t.requireOk('ToDoListApp.model.Task', function() {
    var task = Ext.create('ToDoListApp.model.Task', {
        title: 'Buy milk',
        description: 'This is a test task',
        completed: true,
        dueDate: new Date()
    });

    t.is(task.get('title'), 'Buy milk', 'title works ok');
    t.is(task.get('description'), 'This is a test task',
    'Could read description');
    t.ok(task.get('completed'), 'The task is completed');
    t.isNot(task.get('dueDate'), null, 'The task date must not be null');
    });
});
```

Siesta includes a number of useful assertions that can be used to test the state of different parts of the code:

- `t.is()` takes three parameters and verifies the identity or equality of the first two operands. As you might imagine, `t.isNot()` performs the inverse operation.

- `t.ok()` verifies that a particular statement is `true`. Of course, `t.notOk()` does exactly the opposite.

Many other functions are provided by Siesta to allow developers to script the expected actions of their applications:

- `t.requireOk()` is used to load asynchronously required classes, and to perform a function once the code is loaded.

- `t.chain()` is used to execute a sequence of asynchronous operations, having Siesta waiting for the end of the current operation before starting a new one.

- `t.waitForCQ()` expects a particular element to be rendered and available in the DOM before executing a callback function.

Siesta documentation

Siesta contains a full documentation set (created using JSDuck) in the bryntum.com website (*http://www.bryntum.com/docs/siesta/#!/api/ Siesta.Test.SenchaTouch*).

To see these functions in play, check the source code repository for this book; in the "Testing and Debugging" folder, you are going to find examples that cover these methods.

Figure 8-13 shows the iOS browser after all the tests have been executed. This screen details the number of tests that have been executed, including the number of failed and passed tests.

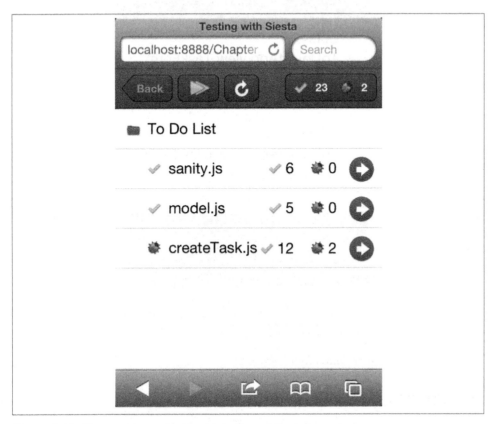

Figure 8-13. Siesta output after the execution of the tests

Developers can inspect the individual status of each test, as shown in Figure 8-14.

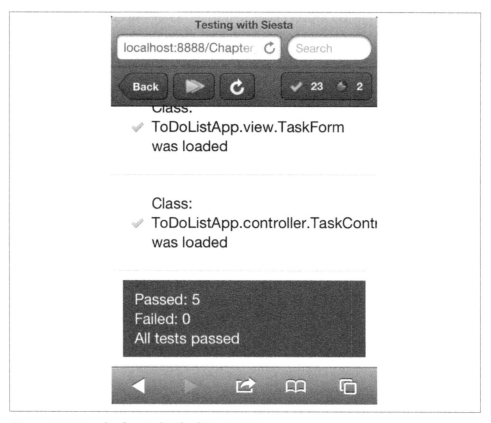

Figure 8-14. Result of an individual Siesta test

Documenting Your Code with JSDuck

In Chapter 1, you read about the amazing documentation tool provided by Sencha Touch. As another major contribution to the open-source world, Sencha has released the source code of the underlying tool used to generate this documentation set, and it is called JSDuck (*https://github.com/senchalabs/jsduck*).

You can easily install JSDuck using RubyGems (*http://rubygems.org/*), the standard package manager for the Ruby community, using the following command:

```
gem install jsduck
```

This will install the required dependencies automatically.

Installing JSDuck in Mountain Lion

If the installation of JSDuck fails under Mountain Lion (something that happened while writing this chapter), you might want to try the following set of commands, borrowed from a Ruby forum thread (*http://www.ruby-forum.com/topic/4306127*):

```
$ gem uninstall libv8
    --> select all versions!
$ gem install therubyracer
$ gem install jsduck
```

The preceding commands should normally fix the problem.

Once JSDuck is installed, you should start adding documentation tags to your code. If you browse the source code of the AkoLib.view.SplitView class (included in the source code of this book in Github (*https://github.com/akosma/Sencha-Touch-2-Up-And-Running*)) you will see a set of documentation tags, very similar to those of Javadoc (*http://en.wikipedia.org/wiki/Javadoc*), Doxygen (*http://doxygen.org*), or similar code documentation tools.

To begin with, you can add a header to your classes, showing examples of how to use your components, including dependencies or other interesting information:

```
/**
 * Basic class for creating a component similar to the
 * UISplitViewController in the iPad.
 *
 * This component requires two components to work:
 *
 * - On the left side, the `masterView` usually contains a list of
 *   objects.
 * - On the right side, the `detailView` displays the details of the
 *   item selected on the `masterView`.
 *
 * To use it, include the `AkoLib` in your project:
 *
 *     Ext.Loader.setConfig({
 *         paths: {
 *             'AkoLib': '../AkoLib'
 *         }
 *     });
 *
 * Then configure a new instance of it and add it to your Viewport, typically
 * inside the profile for tablets or desktop apps:
 *
 *     Ext.Viewport.add({
 *         xtype: 'akosplitview',
 *         screenTitle: 'Universal App',
 *         menuButtonTitle: 'Menu',
 *         masterView: {
 *             xtype: 'indexview'
```

```
 *          },
 *          detailView: {
 *              xtype: 'panel',
 *              html: 'Select an item in the menu'
 *          }
 *      });
 *
 */
Ext.define('AkoLib.view.SplitView', {
    extend: 'Ext.Container',
    xtype: 'akosplitview',
    config: {
```

Developers can then document the individual `config` parameters of the class:

```
/**
 * @cfg {Object} [detailView=null]
 * The Component instance to be displayed on the right-hand side
 * of the split view.
 */
detailView: null,

/**
 * @cfg {String} [screenTitle="Sample Split View"]
 * The default title shown when the split view is initialized.
 */
screenTitle: 'Sample Split View',

/**
 * @cfg {Array} [detailToolbarButtons=null]
 * An array of buttons that are added to the toolbar on top of
 * the detail component.
 */
detailToolbarButtons: null,

/**
 * @cfg {Boolean} [collapsesMasterView=true]
 * A flag that indicates whether the component can collapse
 * its master view or not.
 */
collapsesMasterView: true,
```

The different events fired by the component can also be exposed:

```
/**
 * @event masterviewhide
 * Fires whenever the master view has been hidden
 * @param {AkoLib.view.SplitView} this The component instance
 */
/**
 * @event beforemasterviewshow
 * Fires whenever the master view is about to be shown
```

```
 * @param {AkoLib.view.SplitView} this The component instance
 */
```

And last, but not least, the documentation tags for methods, both public and private:

```
/**
 * Sets the title of the current split view.
 * @param {String} title The new title for the split view.
 */
setTitle: function (title) {
    var toolbar = this.getTitleToolbar();
    toolbar.setTitle(title);
},

/**
 * Sets the component to be displayed inside the detail view.
 * @param {Ext.Component} component The component to be displayed.
 */
displayComponent: function (component) {
    var contentPanel = this.getContentPanel();
    contentPanel.removeAll(false, false);
    contentPanel.add(component);
    this.hideOverlayView();
},

/**
 * Returns a pointer to the content panel, located inside the
 * detail panel.
 * @private
 */
getContentPanel: function () {
    if (!this.contentPanel) {
        this.contentPanel = this.getDetailPanel().getComponent('contentPanel');
    }
    return this.contentPanel;
},
```

Once the code is documented, the `jsduck` command generates the set of HTML files with the documentation set:

```
jsduck AkoLib/view/SplitView.js --external Ext.Component --output docs
```

The resulting HTML looks identical to the official Sencha Touch documentation set, as shown in Figure 8-15; it includes all the standard functionality provided by the standard documentation, including live searching and filtering, menus, and tree structure.

Figure 8-15. Documentation generated by JSDuck

 For another nice example of documentation generated by JSDuck take a look at the Siesta documentation site (*http://www.bryntum.com/docs/ siesta/#!/api/Siesta.Test.SenchaTouch*).

Tips for Quality Sencha Touch Apps

You might find the following guidelines useful when developing and debugging Sencha Touch apps:

- Use a tool such as JSLint (*http://www.jslint.com/*) or JSHint (*http:// www.jshint.com/*) to continuously deliver quality JavaScript code. The best approach is to use it every time you save your JavaScript files, and many IDEs and code editors allow you to do that. Check the documentation of your favorite tool!

- Use a continuous approach when writing your code. Make small changes in your code, and test them in your browser as soon as possible. This will help you spot problems as soon as you have written a particular line of code, instead of after having written hundreds of them. The ideal setup is to have your editor window next to your browser, and as soon as your files are saved, to refresh the browser window immediately. To makes things easier, use a tool such as LiveReload (*http://livere*

load.com/), which works brilliantly when using several monitors. You can edit your code on one screen, have your browser in another, and as soon as you save your file, your modifications are immediately visible.

- Test your code in real devices; many bugs and performance issues are visible only when running the application in a real device, so you should be aware of those as soon as possible. If you are using LiveReload, you can have many devices connected to your workstation and see them being refreshed automatically every time you save your files. You can also use Adobe Edge Inspect or the remote debugging capabilities of iOS 6, Safari 6, or OS X Mountain Lion to help you in this task.

- Commit early and often to your source code repository. This is particularly important when working in teams.

- Use the MVC structure proposed and enforced by Sencha Touch. Even for small applications, it is totally worth it.

- Use unit tests for the most critical sections of your code; remember the Pareto Principle (*http://en.wikipedia.org/wiki/Pareto_principle*): "80% of the benefits come from 20% of the effort." Find that 20% critical section of your code and document and test it. Do it for the rest of your project only if you have the budget and time to do it.

- Reuse code. Create a small library (like the AkoLib library provided in the code samples for this book) and reuse it in your projects. The best libraries consist of code that has been put into production in previous applications, so do not hesitate to reuse classes and components if required.

- If you are going to reuse code, remember to document it using JSDuck, and even test it, if required.

Finally, to make your life simpler during development, you can use this trick to enable mouse scrolling support in Sencha Touch applications (*http://bit.ly/12sUqV7*) (because, as you might have experienced, it is not possible to scroll lists or other scrollable components using your mouse!):

```
// Native scrolling in browser
document.addEventListener('mousewheel', function (e) {
    var el = e.target;
    var results = [];
    while (el !== document.body) {
        if (el && el.className && el.className.indexOf('x-container') >= 0) {
            var cmp = Ext.getCmp(el.id);
            if (cmp &&
                typeof cmp.getScrollable == 'function' &&
                cmp.getScrollable()) {
                var scroller = cmp.getScrollable().getScroller();
                if (scroller) {
                    var offset = {
                        x: 0,
```

```
                    y: -e.wheelDelta * 0.5
                };
                scroller.fireEvent('scrollstart',
                                    scroller,
                                    scroller.position.x,
                                    scroller.position.y,
                                    e);
                scroller.scrollBy(offset.x, offset.y);
                scroller.snapToBoundary();
                scroller.fireEvent('scrollend',
                                    scroller,
                                    scroller.position.x,
                                    scroller.position.y - offset.y);
                break;
            }
        }
    }
    results.push(el = el.parentNode);
    }
    return results;
}, false);
```

The preceding script is included in the AkoLib/scripts folder in the source code repository of this book in Github (*https://github.com/akosma/Sencha-Touch-2-Up-And-Running*).

Conclusion

In this chapter we have seen how to use several different technologies to debug, test, and document our code before shipping it. The WebKit Inspector can be used to increase the quality of our applications, and it can be accessed in many different ways, both locally and remotely. Siesta and Jasmine constitute enterprise-level testing frameworks, which can be used to verify and certify the quality of any application. Finally, JSDuck enables your team to document the code of your applications, to be able to generate useful documentation sets for the team to refer to.

## CHAPTER 9

Sencha Architect

During the past few chapters, we have crafted the user interface of our applications, using the common `items` and `xtype` properties in both parent and child views. In this chapter we are going to learn about Sencha Architect, a full fledged user interface designer and IDE designed to simplify the creation of complex projects based on Sencha Touch or Ext JS.

Introduction

Sencha Architect is a cross-platform desktop application, running on Windows, Linux, and OS X, that allows developers and designers to quickly draft, prototype, and create user interfaces based on both Ext JS and Sencha Touch. It can be downloaded from the Sencha Architect home page (*http://www.sencha.com/products/architect*) as shown in Figure 9-1.

 At the time of this writing, the latest available version of Sencha Architect is 2.1.0 (build 676).

iOS and .NET developers will immediately feel at home using Sencha Architect, because this tool provides a similar experience to that of Interface Builder (now integrated into Xcode) or the classic Visual Studio designer experience.

Figure 9-1. Sencha Architect download page

But Sencha Architect allows developers to do much more than just craft an elegant UI in a few mouse clicks; Sencha Architect actually supports the whole MVC architecture of Sencha Touch and Ext JS, and it allows you to visually define and customize the following types of objects:

- Models, including relationships, fields, data types, and other characteristics
- Stores, of array or tree types
- Views, including forms and complex containers
- Controllers, with their `refs`, `control`, `routes` and event handler functions

With Sencha Architect, very complex applications can be created in a few mouse clicks, ready to be customized and personalized. Even better, Sencha Architect generates high-quality JavaScript code, easy to understand and to customize afterward.

Installation

Sencha Architect is available through a commercial license, as it is not an open-source application. It is available as a standalone download from the Sencha website, and it is also available as part of the yearly developer subscriptions, including support and new releases.

Sencha Architect runs on Windows, OS X, and Linux, generating the same project files and JavaScript code on each platform, ensuring cross-platform support. It requires and generates applications running only under Sencha Touch 2.0 or higher, and Ext JS 4.0 or higher.

 Sencha Architect can be downloaded and used for 30 days with a free trial license. To use it for free during the trial period, you need a Sencha Forums account, which can be created for free directly from the Sencha Architect welcome screen, as shown in Figure 9-2.

Figure 9-2. Creating a Sencha Forums ID directly from Sencha Architect

Sencha Architect is distributed with an easy-to-use installer that will perform all the required operations to get the software up and running in your workstation.

User Interface

When Sencha Architect is launched, it displays the welcome screen shown in Figure 9-3, allowing the user to open a previous project or to create a new one, in either Sencha Touch or Ext JS.

Figure 9-3. Sencha Architect welcome screen

After the user chooses to create a new project using Sencha Touch 2.1, the screen shown in Figure 9-4 appears.

Figure 9-4. Sencha Architect main window

The Sencha Architect window is divided into four sections (the numbers correspond to those used in Figure 9-4):

1. The **toolbar** on top provides access to the most common project manipulation options available.

2. The leftmost pane contains the **toolbox**, offering a menu of different components, arranged in categories, and with a filter search box on top, to allow users to quickly find the components they are looking for. The toolbox contains not only visual components such as toolbars or buttons, but also models, stores, and even graph configuration objects, which can be dragged and dropped on top of the application canvas.

3. The center pane contains the **canvas**, where the developer can craft the UI of her application, and also modify the source code if required, using the Design/Code switch on top. At the bottom of the canvas, a drop-down list (shown in Figure 9-5) allows the developer to switch among simulated devices (with choices such as iPhone, iPad, Google Nexus S, Playbook, Kindle Fire, and even the possibility of defining your own sizes). A switch also allows you to toggle between the

portrait and landscape orientations, as well as to zoom in and out (particularly useful when simulating large tablets).

4. The rightmost pane contains, on top, the **Project Inspector**, which displays the MVC structure of the project, including stores and resources.

5. On the bottom-right side of the screen, the **Attribute Inspector** allows the manipulation of the internal structure of any object selected either on the canvas or in the Project Inspector.

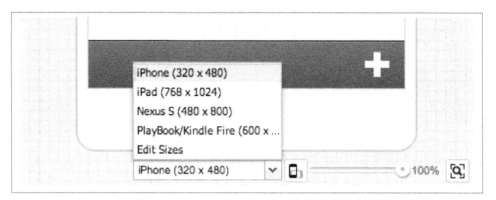

Figure 9-5. Simulating different device sizes on the canvas

In the following sections, we are going to see how to create a simple application, and the discussion will refer to the UI elements highlighted in the previous paragraphs.

Creating a Simple Application

Sencha Architect is a rather large application, worthy of a whole book; in this chapter we are going to provide a short introduction to it, creating from scratch the To Do list application that was created initially for Chapter 8.

Configuring the Application

The first step whenever you create a new Sencha Architect project is to save it in a convenient location, and to provide an application name for it. Remember that, as we saw in Chapter 1, the name of the application is used as the base namespace for all the classes required by the application, and loaded by the Ext.Loader infrastructure, so it must not contain spaces.

To provide a name for your application, click the Application object in your Project Inspector, and then scroll the Attributes Inspector until you find the name property;

change its value from MyApp (which is the default value) to ToDoList, as shown in Figure 9-6.

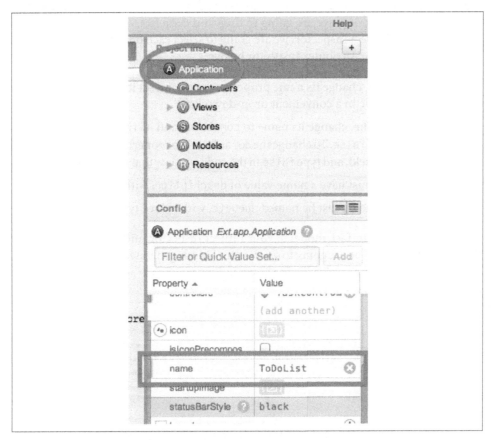

Figure 9-6. Changing the name of the application

You can change several high-level properties for your application at this moment, such as the startupImage, statusBarStyle, or icon properties.

Creating a Model Class

We are going to start working on our application at the "lowest" layers of the MVC architecture: the models and the stores. The first step will be the definition of a model class for our application, conveniently called Task.

To do that, filter the toolbox by clicking on the Data category, and then select, from the Data Models group, a model object, and drag and drop it to the Models node in your

Project Inspector. In the Attributes Inspector, select the userClassName attribute and change its value to Task.

We are going to follow a similar workflow to add fields to our model class; in the toolbox, in the Data Models group, we are going to drag and drop four field objects on top of our model in the Project Inspector; we are going to select each one of them, and change their properties in the Attributes Inspector below:

- For the first field, change its name property to title, and set its type to string (you can select the type in a convenient drop-down list.)

- For the second one, change its name to completed and its type to boolean, with a defaultValue of false. To change the defaultValue property, click the Edit button in the inspector field, and type false in the code window that appears on the canvas.

- The third field must have a name value of description, with a type of string.

- Finally, the last field must be named dueDate, with a date type.

If you click now on the Task model in your Project Inspector, and then select the Code switch on the canvas, you are going to see the source code generated by Sencha Architect, representing our own model class, as shown in Figure 9-7.

Figure 9-7. Model definition

Creating a Store

Having defined our model, we are going to do the same operation to create a suitable store. In the Data category of the toolbox, scroll down until you see the Data Stores section; select a Store object from the toolbox and drag it to the Stores item in your Project Inspector.

Configure the store in the Attributes Inspector with the following properties:

- `userClassName: TaskStore`
- `autoLoad: true`
- `autoSync: true`
- `model: Task` (you can select the proper model from a drop-down list)
- `storeId: TaskStore` (this value will be used by the `Ext.data.StoreManager` singleton, remember?)

Adding a proxy

As you might remember from Chapter 4, stores delegate the choice of the underlying storage strategy to proxies; in our case, we are going to select a LocalStorage Proxy from the Data Proxies group in the toolbox and drag it on top of our newly added store object in the Project Inspector. Then make sure your proxy is selected and change the `id` property in the Attributes Inspector, using the `senchatasks` value.

Adding sorters and groupers

Just like in the previous step, we can add sorting and grouping options to our store in a few clicks. In the toolbox, select a Sorter object (from the Data Utilities group) and configure it as follows:

- `displayName: dueDateSorter`
- `direction: ASC`
- `property: dueDate`

Next, select a Grouper object in the toolbox, drop it on your store object in the Project Inspector, and configure it in the Attributes Inspector as follows:

- `displayName: dueDateGrouper`
- `sortProperty: dueDate`

The final property we are going to configure in our grouper is the `groupFn` property, which will expose you to the integrated code editor of Sencha Architect; just click the

Edit button next to the `groupFn` property, and this will display an empty code editor section on the canvas. This code editor features syntax highlighting of JavaScript code, and even includes integrated JSHint (*http://www.jshint.com/*) functionality to highlight common errors, as shown in Figure 9-8.

```
tap saveTask  ▾   Create Override          ⬆  📋   Design   Code

        saveTask: function(button, e, options) {
33   var store = this.getTaskList().getStore();
34   var task = this.getTaskForm().getRecord();
35   this.getTaskForm().updateRecord(task);
36
37   // Is it a new object?
38   if (null === store.findRecord("id", task.get('id'))) {
39       store.add(task);
40   }
41
42   this.showList()
43
┌─────────────────┐
│ Missing semicolon.│
└─────────────────┘
```

Figure 9-8. JSHint integration

The `TaskStore` class for our project should look like Figure 9-9, which also displays the "edit" button that appears on the gutter of the Canvas when hovering with the mouse on top of a JavaScript function. Clicking on that button opens up an editor window that allows the code to be edited inside of Sencha Architect.

Figure 9-9. Store definition

Creating Views and Forms

Arguably the most interesting task that can be performed on Sencha Architect is the creation and manipulation of view components. Developers can create complex component hierarchies just by dragging and dropping components on top of one another.

The procedure is very similar to what we have seen so far; grab the component from the toolbox, drag it on top of the Views node on the Project Inspector (or, alternatively, on top of the canvas) and configure its properties using the Attributes Inspector. In the case of our To Do List application, we are going to perform the following tasks:

1. Drag a Navigation View on the canvas

   - Configure it, setting the `autoDestroy` property to `false` (the property is `true` by default.)

2. Drag a List on the Navigation View created in the previous step.

   - Configure the list to use the `TaskStore` store, and to have its `grouped` and `onItemDisclosure` properties set to `true`. Also, set its `title` property to To Do List.

3. Drag a Toolbar object on top of the list.

   - Set its `docked` property to `bottom`.

4. Drag a Spacer object on top of the toolbar created above.

5. Drag a Button on top of the toolbar.

   - Set its `iconCls` property to `add`, and its `ui` property to `plain`. Also, remove the contents of the `text` property. Finally, add a custom property named `action` with the value `createTask`. Sencha Architect allows you to add as many properties as required, including those that are not included by default in the framework.

A similar procedure will be used to create the task form shown in Figure 9-10.

 In Figure 9-10 also shows the icon used by Sencha Architect (at the rightmost edge of the screen, next to the `RootNavView` navigation view) to indicate the view that is displayed on application startup. This parameter can be changed in the Attributes Inspector, thanks to the `initialView` property.

Figure 9-10. Form editor

Adding a CSS resource

To spice up our design, we can also add a supplementary CSS file to our application; in the Resources group of the toolbox, grab a CSS Resource object and drag it to the Resources node in the Project Inspector. Change its `url` property in the Attributes Inspector to `styles.css`, and Sencha Architect will automatically generate a new file in the application, as well as including it in the `app.html` file. Any styles added to this file will be used automatically in your application as well.

Creating Controllers

The final piece in the MVC puzzle is controllers. As usual, editing them in Sencha Architect involves building them, piece by piece, including all the elements described in Chapter 6: `refs`, `control`, `routes`, and event handler functions.

The toolbox contains controller-related objects in the Behaviors category. The first thing to do will be to grab a Controller object and to drag it to the Controllers node of the Project Inspector. The only attribute that must be changed in this case is the `userClass Name`, this time set to `TaskController`.

Creating refs

We are going to add a refs entry, represented by Controller Reference objects on the toolbox. Drag and drop one and set its properties as follows:

- displayName: createTaskButton
- ref: createTaskButton
- selector: button[action=createTask]

As explained in Chapter 6, each entry in the refs object will have its getter function automatically generated; in the case above, we will be able to get a reference to this button anywhere in the controller functions, thanks to the this.getCreateTaskButton() function.

Creating control entries

Now we have to add a control entry, which binds a refs entry to any event handlers defined in the controller. To do that, just grab a Controller Action object from the toolbox, drag it on top of the TaskController object created previously on the Project Inspector, and set its properties as follows in the Attributes Inspector:

- controlQuery: createTaskButton
- targetType: Ext.Button (you can select this value from a drop-down list)
- fn: createTask
- name: tap (this event name is also provided by a drop-down list)

Because JavaScript variables can have any type, we have to tell Sencha Architect manually about the targetType of our object; this enables the tool to filter the events exposed by a particular component class, and it also provides us with the complete list of parameters for its handler functions.

Populating an event handler

By setting the parameters above in the definition of our controller action, Sencha Architect will create an empty createTask JavaScript function with the proper parameters corresponding to a tap event handler; by selecting the Code view in the canvas, we can click that function and set its code to be the following:

```
Ext.Msg.alert('createTask', 'On the create task tap handler!');
```

Run the application, click the + button appearing at the bottom of the list, and you should see an alert box appear on screen. The actual code of the event handler will perform more meaningful tasks (creating a task, attaching it to the form, and displaying the form) but this is shown in detail in the source code repository in Github (*https://github.com/akosma/Sencha-Touch-2-Up-And-Running*).

In any case, repeating this sequence of steps will gradually populate your controller with all the required logic to handle tasks in your application, as shown in Figure 9-11.

Figure 9-11. Editing controllers

Working with Projects

Sencha Architect enables a series of very useful operations on projects, for example:

- Saving snapshot images of UI elements
- Creating a new component in the toolbox
- Previewing your application in a browser
- Publishing your application to a web server

Saving snapshots

By clicking on the Snapshot button on the toolbar (or selecting the View → Snap Screenshot… menu item) you will be prompted to save the currently visible components on the canvas, on any simulated device or size, as a PNG file in the location of your choice. This can be very useful to share with your team, as you move forward in the development of your application, showing the current state of the application in different sizes.

Adding components to the toolbox

This is a really neat feature; by selecting the Actions → Save to Toolbox… menu entry, the user is prompted to save the currently selected UI component on the canvas as a reusable object in the toolbox. Figure 9-12 shows the dialog presented to the user when trying to save the TaskForm component created in the previous sections as an object on the toolbox.

Figure 9-12. Saving a component in the toolbox

Previewing an application

Anytime during the development of your application, you can click the Preview button on the toolbar (or use the File → Preview Project... menu entry) and open a browser window. The first time this functionality is invoked, the user can enter the URL where the project can be seen (assuming, of course, that the project is hosted and available through a local or remote web server).

Figure 9-13. Previewing an application

Publishing an application

Finally, when developers want to deploy their applications, they can invoke the Publish button in the toolbar (or, alternatively, use the File → Publish Project... menu entry) and copy the required files to a local or remote web server; the first time this functionality is invoked, Architect asks for the path where the files should be deployed, as shown in Figure 9-14.

About packaging applications
Readers might have noticed a Package button in the toolbar as well; this functionality will be described in detail in Chapter 10.

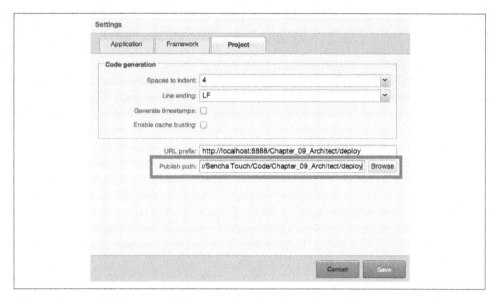

Figure 9-14. Publishing an application

Conclusion

The final application, completely created from scratch using Sencha Architect, can be found in the source code of this book in Github (*https://github.com/akosma/Sencha-Touch-2-Up-And-Running*).

Sencha Architect is a commercial application that provides a great environment geared toward rapid application development. It allows developers to quickly craft user interfaces using visual tools, but it also provides a complete integration of the whole MVC architecture. It allows you to design not only the UI of an application, but actually every single aspect of it, including models, stores, and controllers.

Developers, designers, and enterprise architects can use this tool to create and customize complex applications in a fraction of the time required to create the same systems manually. Sencha Architect generates clean, easy-to-read code that is also easily extensible by the developer team.

## CHAPTER 10

Deployment in Devices

Sencha Touch apps are by no means limited to live their lives exclusively in a browser; developers can deploy their creations also as native iOS and/or Android applications to their respective marketplaces.

To make the experience richer for the end user, Sencha Touch applications can access a large selection of native device APIs, including connectivity, location, and orientation information. Even better, Sencha Touch applications can detect whether they run in a tablet, a smartphone, or a desktop environment, and change their appearance in a very convenient way, using a feature named "profiles."

This last chapter will provide an overview of the tasks required to get your applications running as native applications!

Using Profiles

Mobile devices such as tablets and smartphones have different screen sizes, and they are used in different contexts; however, mobile applications have to share code and resources to make them look alike and to have similar and consistent behavior across devices. As such, it is nice to know that Sencha Touch provides profiles, which allow developers to offer different user experiences in different device categories.

 Nearly all the applications included in the source code of this book, hosted in Github (*https://github.com/akosma/Sencha-Touch-2-Up-And-Running*), use profiles by default and offer different user interfaces in different contexts.

Adding Profiles

Profiles are implemented through the `Ext.app.Profile` class. Applications use this class in the standard `app.js` file, as entries in the `profiles` key:

```
Ext.application({
    name: 'Chapter10Profiles',
    profiles: ['Phone', 'Tablet', 'Desktop'],

    // ...

    launch: function () {
        // ...
    }
});
```

When the application above starts, Sencha Touch will load the files located in the following locations: *app/profile/Phone.js*, *app/profile/Tablet.js*, and *app/profile/Desktop.js*. Each of these files should contain a similarly named class, inheriting from `Ext.app.Pro file`:

```
Ext.define('Chapter10Profiles.profile.Phone', {
    extend: 'Ext.app.Profile',
    config: {
        name: 'SamplePhone'
    },
    isActive: function () {
        return Ext.os.is.Phone; // ❶
    },
    launch: function () {
        // ...
    }
});
```

❶ Subclasses of `Ext.app.Profile` should implement this method, which in the base class returns `false` by default. The usual implementation involves, as shown above, asking about the current environment (operating system, browser, and so on).

The profile classes are all loaded at once; their `isActive()` functions are called in no particular order. The first profile that returns `true` is the one that will be active, and the evaluation of the other profiles is stopped at that point. That is why it is important to know that the `isActive()` function calls can happen in any order, particularly when an application contains several profiles returning `true` in a certain context.

It is very common to have two profiles in applications, one for smart-phones and another shared by tablets and desktop browsers. However, the profile system allows for maximum flexibility, and developers can adapt it to any situation.

Initialization Functions

In Chapter 6 you read about how the application startup process works; there is a particular sequence of function calls happening when an application starts, and of course profiles are part of this equation as well. In particular, profiles can define their own launch() functions, allowing developers to provide different behaviors in different devices.

The sequence of calls is the following:

1. All the controllers execute their init() functions first.
2. Then the current profile (the first one that returned true from isActive(), as explained above) executes its own launch() function.
3. After that, the main launch() function (defined in the *app.js* file) is executed.
4. Finally, the individual launch() functions defined in each controller are executed.

This is useful to bootstrap different UIs for tablets and phones; for example, you can use the AkoLib.view.SplitView class introduced in Chapter 3 when loading your application in a tablet or a desktop browser and use a different approach on phones altogether. The launch() function defined in the *app.js* file is also executed, allowing for sharing initialization code among devices.

Custom MVC Classes

In addition to specifying its own launch() function, each profile can include its own set of model, view, and controller entries, each extending the functionality specified in the *app.js* file.

```
Ext.define('Chapter10Profiles.profile.Phone', {
    extend: 'Ext.app.Profile',
    config: {
        name: 'SamplePhone',
        models: [],
        views: ['PhoneView'], // ❶
        controllers: []
    },
    isActive: function () {
        return Ext.os.is.Phone;
    },
```

```
    launch: function () {
        Ext.Viewport.add({
            xtype: 'phoneview' // ❷
        });
    }
});
```

❶ This entry prompts the class loader to include the `Chapter10Profiles.view.sam
    plephone.PhoneView` in the current application. The location of the file should
    be *app/view/samplephone/PhoneView.js*, as expected, and the `samplephone` part
    comes from the fact that the `name` parameter in the configuration of the profile
    is `SamplePhone`.

❷ This `xtype` corresponds to the `PhoneView` class, specified in the preceding `views`
    collection.

The same naming conventions apply to models and controllers, as expected.

Using Device Features

Sencha Touch applications running as native ones might require access to extended
functionality, such as the following:

- Learning about the capabilities of the current device
- Access the camera or the photo library
- Using native notification options
- Handling orientation changes
- Managing network connectivity
- Getting location information

The following section explains which APIs are available in Sencha Touch to help in these
situations.

What about contacts?
At the time of this writing, the official word from the Sencha team is
that there exists an API to access the contacts stored in the device, using
the `Ext.device.Contacts` object. However, although the API is available and documented, it does not appear to work in a live example. The
source code of the sample applications for this book in Github (*https://
github.com/akosma/Sencha-Touch-2-Up-And-Running*) will be updated as soon as possible to include an example of this API, but this chapter
does not include a discussion of it.

Device Capabilities

In "Ext.env.Feature" (page 50), you saw how to use the `Ext.env.Feature` class to learn about the capabilities of the current system where the application is running:

```
var key = null;
var value = false;
var text = '';
console.log('Available features:');
for (key in Ext.feature.has) { // ❶
    value = Ext.feature.has[key];
    text = key + ': ' + value;
    console.log(text);
}
```

❶ `Ext.feature` is the singleton instance of the `Ext.env.Feature` class.

The execution of the code above could yield the following output:

```
Available features:
Canvas: true
Svg: true
Vml: true
Touch: false
Orientation: false
OrientationChange: false
...
```

Accessing the Camera

To access the camera, Sencha exposes the `Ext.device.Camera` API, which can be used as shown here:

```
loadCamera: function (button, e, eOpts) {
    var self = this;

    Ext.device.Camera.capture({
        source: 'camera',
        destination: 'file',

        success: function(url) {
            self.getImage().setSrc(url);
        }
    });
}
```

Changing the `source` parameter to `library` prompts the user to choose an image from the local image library instead of the camera.

Accessing the camera or the photo library is a security risk; in iOS 6 or higher, users are prompted before allowing the application to access them, and in Android, your application should request the appropriate permissions in the manifest XML file.

Native Notifications and Vibration

You learned in Chapter 3 about the powerful asynchronous notifications provided by Sencha Touch in the `Ext.Msg` singleton object; however, to provide a stronger native look and feel to your application, you can access the native alerts provided by the operating system instead. To do that, just use the `Ext.device.Notification.show()` method, as shown in the following code:

```
Ext.device.Notification.show({
    title: 'Native notification',
    message: 'This is a native notification',
    buttons: ['Red', 'Yellow', 'Green'],

    callback: function(answer) {
        button.getParent().down('#mainLabel').setHtml('Touched button: '
        + answer);
    }
});
```

In iOS, this notification appears as shown in Figure 10-1.

Figure 10-1. Native iOS notification

To trigger a vibration of your device, just use this simple code:

```
Ext.device.Notification.vibrate();
```

Orientation Changes

The Ext.device.Orientation object triggers the orientationchange event, which can be handled just like any other Sencha Touch event; the function that works as event handler receives an event object as parameter, with the alpha, beta, and gamma parameters. The W3C DeviceOrientation Event Specification (*http://dev.w3.org/geo/api/spec-source-orientation.html#deviceorientation*) explains in detail what these parameters mean:

> The alpha, beta, and gamma attributes of the event must specify the orientation of the device in terms of the transformation from a coordinate frame fixed on the Earth to a coordinate frame fixed in the device. The coordinate frames must be oriented as described below.
>
> The Earth coordinate frame is a *East, North, Up* frame at the user's location. It has the following 3 axes, where the ground plane is tangent to the spheroid of the World Geodetic System 1984, at the user's location.
>
> - East (X) is in the ground plane, perpendicular to the North axis and positive towards the East.
> - North (Y) is in the ground plane and positive towards True North (towards the North Pole).
> - Up (Z) is perpendicular to the ground plane and positive upwards.
>
> — W3C DeviceOrientation Event Specification

The following code shows how to use the device orientation information in your app:

```
Ext.device.Orientation.on('orientationchange', function(e) {
    var alpha = Math.round(e.alpha);
    var beta = Math.round(e.beta);
    var gamma = Math.round(e.gamma);
    var text = [alpha, beta, gamma].join(", ");

    console.log('Orientation changed: ' + text);
    self.setHtml('Orientation changed: ' + text);
});
```

Network Connectivity

The Ext.device.Connection object contains two useful methods that can be used to get information about the current network connection of the device:

- isOnline() returns a self-describing Boolean value
- getType() returns a string with a textual description of the current network conditions.

You can also hook yourself to the onlinechange event to be notified live of any new networking condition experienced by your device.

Pay attention to false positives and negatives!
This information relies on rather shaky heuristics to detect the network status of the current device; as a matter of fact, a device can be online (which usually means having an assigned IP address and a routing connection) without a real connection to the Internet (which actually depends on many other factors, usually out of reach of the user).

So, whenever this API reports that the device is "online," remember to add the proper fallback code, in case your network requests are dropped or fail to return the required information.

The getType() function returns one of the following string constants:

- UNKNOWN: 'Unknown connection'
- ETHERNET: 'Ethernet connection'
- WIFI: 'WiFi connection'
- CELL_2G: 'Cell 2G connection'
- CELL_3G: 'Cell 3G connection'
- CELL_4G: 'Cell 4G connection'
- NONE: 'No network connection'

The code below shows how to use this API:

```
if (Ext.device.Connection.isOnline()) {
    this.setHtml('Connected (' + Ext.device.Connection.getType() + ')');
} else {
    this.setHtml('Disconnected');
}
```

Location Information

The final API we are going to see in this section is the Ext.device.Geolocation object, which provides Sencha Touch applications with information about the current latitude, longitude, altitude, speed, and compass heading of the current device.

There are two functions available in `Ext.device.Geolocation`, both very similar in terms of parameters and outcome:

`getCurrentPosition()`
> Performs a one-time call

`watchPosition()`
> Calls the `success` event handler periodically with the information of the current position as the user moves around

The following code shows how to use these API functions:

```
initialize: function () {
    this.callParent(arguments);
    var self = this;

    Ext.device.Geolocation.getCurrentPosition({
        success: function(position) {
            self.showPosition(position.coords);
        },
        failure: function() {
            self.showError();
        }
    });

    Ext.device.Geolocation.watchPosition({
        frequency: 5000,
        success: function(position) {
            self.showPosition(position.coords);
        },
        failure: function() {
            self.showError();
        }
    });
},

showPosition: function (position) {
    var label = this.down('#dataLabel');
    var text = [
        'Accuracy: ' + position.accuracy,
        'Altitude: ' + position.altitude,
        'Altitude accuracy: ' + position.altitudeAccuracy,
        'Heading: ' + position.heading,
        'Latitude: ' + position.latitude,
        'Longitude: ' + position.longitude,
        'Speed: ' + position.speed
    ];
    label.setHtml(text.join('<br>'));
},

showError: function () {
    var label = this.down('#dataLabel');
```

```
        label.setHtml('Could not retrieve location');
    }
```

Include your success and failure callbacks

If things can go wrong, they will; so be sure to include your success and failure callbacks, not only when using the Ext.device.Geoloca tion API but also with any other device API, and provide feedback to the user whenever possible if your application cannot provide the service requested by the user.

Packaging with Sencha Cmd

We briefly talked about Sencha Cmd in Chapter 1. In this section, we are going to learn to use these tools to perform the following operations:

- Create standalone applications
- Create workspaces
- Package applications as HTML5 apps
- Package and run applications in a simulator or a device

The installation of Sencha Cmd is covered in "Installing Sencha Cmd" (page 7), in Chapter 1.

Creating Standalone Apps

You can create standalone applications using Sencha Cmd using the following command in your terminal:

```
$ sencha -sdk _libs/sencha generate app NewApp ./NewAppFolder
```

The sencha command requires you to know the location of the Sencha Touch distribution folder (generated when unzipping the archive downloaded from the Sencha website). This can be achieved using the -sdk switch, as shown in the previous code, or just by running the command from the same Sencha Touch distribution folder. This is required so that the generated application references the correct locations of the framework files required for the app to run.

The standalone applications generated by the sencha command already contain the following elements:

- The standard MVC folder structure: *app/model*, *app/controller*, and so on

- A set of JSON and XML files, including metadata used for packaging the application and generating production builds
- A Sass file, ready to be customized as explained in Chapter 7, in the *resources/sass* folder
- A file named *index.html* representing the main HTML file of the application

Creating Workspaces

Workspaces are useful to group a set of related applications together, enabling them to share code or to be deployed in a consistent fashion.

To create a workspace, just type the following command:

```
$ sencha -sdk _libs/sencha generate workspace ./MyWorkspace
```

You can add an external library (such as the AkoLib library provided by the source code of this book, available in Github (*https://github.com/akosma/Sencha-Touch-2-Up-And-Running*)) editing the *.sencha/workspace/sencha.cfg* file in your new workspace and adding a workspace.classpath entry:

```
workspace.build.dir=${workspace.dir}/build/${app.name}
workspace.classpath=${workspace.dir}/AkoLib

touch.dir=${workspace.dir}/touch
workspace.cmd.version=3.0.0.250
```

Then you can generate individual applications inside of the workspace folder, using the same command as explained above for creating standalone apps. However, to enable code sharing inside these individual apps, remember to edit the app.js file in each one and to remove the <debug> and </debug> statements on top of the file. Also, include the shared code library for the Sencha class loader system to work properly:

```
Ext.Loader.setPath({
    'Ext': '../touch/src',
    'Chapter10Device': 'app',
    'AkoLib': '../AkoLib' // ❶
});

Ext.application({
    name: 'Chapter10Device',
    profiles: ['Phone', 'Tablet'],

// ...
```

❶ This line is required for the Ext.Loader class loader to find the files of the AkoLib library.

The source code for this book, available in Github (*https://github.com/ akosma/Sencha-Touch-2-Up-And-Running*), is structured as a work-space so you can access it to inspect its structure.

Packaging Applications

During and after the development process, Sencha Cmd allows developers to package the source code of the application in many different ways.

Test package

To generate a test package, without minified source code (which makes it easier to debug) just type the following command:

```
$ sencha app build testing
```

The result of this command will be contained in a folder named *build/APPNAME/test-ing* (where *APPNAME* is the name of your application, given during the execution of the sencha generate app command). Navigating into this folder and opening the *in-dex.html* folder will display the application running as intended, but the JavaScript files will not be minified, which simplifies the debugging process.

HTML5 package

To generate a production HTML5 application, type the following command:

```
$ sencha app build production
```

This command performs the following tasks:

- It concatenates and minifies all the JavaScript files of the application into a single *app.js* file. This file includes only the required parts of the Sencha Touch distribution (as specified by the requires statements inserted all over the application code), which makes the application faster to download and take up less storage space.

- It creates the *resources/css/app.css* CSS file from the Sass files, and minifies its contents.

- It creates a *cache.appcache* file, which is a valid HTML5 application cache file.

The resulting application (to be found in the build/*APPNAME*/production folder) can be deployed as any other offline HTML5 app, and it will be stored offline by the native browsers of iOS and Android as required.

Native package

Finally, the following command generates a native application, using the information contained in the *packager.json* file:

```
$ sencha app build native
```

The *packager.json* file contains a large amount of metadata that can be configured in order to generate iOS or Android apps and to change their names and behavior as required. Here are the contents of the default *packager.json* file:

```
{
        "applicationName":"My Application",                      ❶
        "applicationId":"com.mycompany.myAppID",                 ❷
        "bundleSeedId":"KPXFEPZ6EF",                             ❸
        "versionString":"1.0",
        "versionCode":"1",
        "icon": {
                "57":"resources/icons/Icon.png",
                "72":"resources/icons/Icon~ipad.png",
                "114":"resources/icons/Icon@2x.png",
                "144":"resources/icons/Icon~ipad@2x.png"
        },
        "inputPath":"./",
        "outputPath":"../build/",
        "configuration":"Debug",                                 ❹
        "platform":"iOSSimulator",                               ❺
        "deviceType":"Universal",                                ❻
        "certificateAlias": "iPhone Developer: John Smith",      ❼
        "certificatePath":"/path/to/certificate.file",
        "certificatePassword":"",
        "provisionProfile":"",
        "sdkPath":"/path/to/android-sdk",                        ❽
        "androidAPILevel":"8",
        "permissions":[
                                        "INTERNET",
                                        "ACCESS_NETWORK_STATE",
                                        "CAMERA",
                                "VIBRATE",
                                "ACCESS_FINE_LOCATION",
                                "ACCESS_COARSE_LOCATION",
                                "CALL_PHONE"],
        "orientations": [
                "portrait",
                "landscapeLeft",
                "landscapeRight",
                "portraitUpsideDown"
        ]
}
```

❶   This is the name of the application icon when the application is installed in the device.

❷   This is the application ID, set through the developer consoles provided by Apple for iOS applications and Google for Android applications.

❸   This parameter must be set for iOS applications, and it has to match the application ID specified in the provisioning profile file downloaded from Apple.

❹   This should be Debug or Production, as required.

❺   This can be iOS, Android, iOSSimulator, or AndroidEmulator. This entry is used by the sencha package run command explained in the next section.

❻   This entry can be iPhone, iPad, or Universal, and is taken into account only by iOS apps.

❼   This entry is not included by default, but it should be added and it should match the entry of the iOS developer certificate downloaded from Apple and installed in the Keychain.

❽   The values sdkPath, androidAPILevel, and permissions are required only for Android applications.

Running Applications in the iOS Simulator

To run an application in the iOS Simulator, follow these steps:

1. You must first package it as either a testing or a production build using the commands shown in the previous sections.

2. Then modify the *packager.json* file as follows:

    -   Modify the inputPath key, pointing to the folder location of the testing or production build.

    -   Also, specify iOSSimulator in the platform key.

3. Finally, type the command below and watch the iOS Simulator starting up and running your application:

    ```
    $ sencha package run -p packager.json
    ```

 Install the Xcode tools or the Android SDK first!
In order for you to run the application in the iOS Simulator or the Android Emulator, please make sure that you install these tools first, and that you configure the Android keys specified in the previous section accordingly.

Running Applications in an iOS Device

To run an application in your iOS device, follow these steps:

You should have a working iOS developer set up and ready before trying these steps. You can deploy applications into a real device only if you are a registered iOS developer with a valid paying subscription. Your computer must have all the required certificates and provisioning profiles installed, too.

1. Edit the following entries in your *packager.json* file:

   - Change `applicationName` and `applicationId` to the entries corresponding to your application.
   - Change `bundleSeedId` to match the application ID prefix used in your provisioning profile.
   - Change `inputPath` to be *build/APPNAME/package*.
   - Change `platform` to `iOS`.

2. Build the application as a native one, using the `sencha app build native` command.
3. Package the app using the `sencha package build -p packager.json` command.
4. Open Xcode and navigate to Window → Organizer. Select the Devices tab in the Organizer.
5. Plug in your iOS device (make sure this device is included in the list of enabled devices in your provisioning profile).
6. Drag the application file located in the *build* folder onto the Applications entry below your device.

The application should be copied into your device, and you should be able to run it like any other native application in your device.

Packaging with Sencha Architect

Sencha Architect, described in detail in Chapter 9, also provides a handy, integrated packaging system.

The first step to package applications using Architect is to configure the project for packaging. Click the Package button on the toolbar, and a configuration dialog should appear, as shown in Figure 10-2:

1. In the "Install plug-ins" entry, set the path of your Sencha Cmd folder (usually *~/bin/Sencha/Cmd/3.0.0.250*) and click the Verify button.

2. On the "Setup project with Cmd" screen, set the path of the Sencha Touch framework that you are using for the project (that is, the folder that was generated after unzipping the framework distribution ZIP file downloaded from Sencha).

3. Finally, in the "Package settings" screen, click the Add Package Settings button.

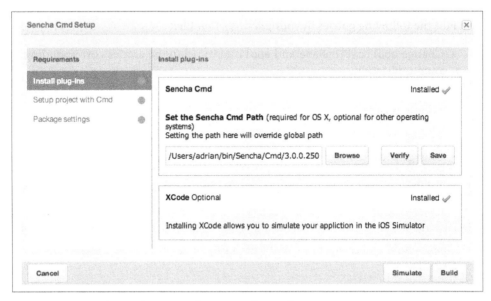

Figure 10-2. Sencha Architect configuration for packaging

Once this is done, click the Simulate button to open the iOS Simulator with the application running, or click the Build button to compile the application as a native one.

Conclusion

Sencha Touch offers a wide array of technical possibilities to get your web applications running as native ones. Profiles allow them to adapt their behavior and appearance in different devices, while the packaging system (available both as command-line tools and as embedded functionality in Sencha Architect) allows developers to deploy them as both HTML5 offline apps or as native iOS and/or Android applications. Finally, the native device APIs can make the final user experience richer and more enjoyable by including real-world data, live in your application.

CHAPTER 11
Conclusion

I sincerely hope that this book has provided you with a good introduction to Sencha Touch, its capabilities, and its possibilities in the realm of modern enterprise mobile web applications. Without a doubt, Sencha Touch 2.1 is, at the time of this writing, one of the most serious options to create complex mobile web apps.

Sencha Touch is available under a flexible licensing scheme, including both GPLv3 and FLOSS licenses for open-source projects, and commercial licenses (free and paid) for companies not willing to be subject to the terms imposed by the GPL, or expecting support for their operations.

Sencha Touch applications can be packaged as native applications, ready to be deployed on the iOS App Store or in any of the available marketplaces for Android, such as Google Play, using the Sencha Cmd tools. Similarly, Sencha Architect provides a serious option for rapid application development of Sencha Touch systems.

Index

Symbols

-skd switch, 15
.NET, 4
.scss extension, 172
10-year period, milliseconds in, 47
\<audio>, 105
\<body>, 31
\<head>, 31
\<html>, 31

A

action sheets, 97
add() function, 44
add() method, 66
Adobe Edge Inspect, 194
Adobe Shadow, 194
ajax proxy, 126
AkoLib.view.SplitView container class, 111
alerts, 98
aliases, 27
Android OS
    Activity root, 93
    addview() method, 18
    audio controls in, 105
    versions supported, 4
    video formats, 106
Android SDK, 246
apostrophes, displaying, 61

append() function, 49
appFolder property, 13, 25
Apple Safari, debugging in, 186
application delegate, 13
applications
    creating basic, 9–14
    creating complex, 215–231
    creating standalone, 242
    creating with command-line tools, 15
    customizing with styles, 171
    entry point for, 11
    folder organization for, 25
    increasing quality of, 212
    previewing, 230
    publishing, 230
    types possible, 2
    typical structure for, 23
Array class, 35
arrays, manipulating, 35
associations, 122
attribute selectors, 49
audio, 105

B

back buttons, 88, 168
base class, choosing, 113
behavior-driven development (BDD), 197
belongsTo property, 122
between() function, 44

We'd like to hear your suggestions for improving our indexes. Send email to index@oreilly.com.

About the Author

Adrian Kosmaczewski has been working as an iOS developer since 2008. Before that, he was a web developer working with classic ASP since 1996, ASP.NET, PHP, Ruby on Rails, Django, and more. He runs a consulting and training business in Oron-la-Ville, Switzerland. He has a master of science degree in information technology from the University of Liverpool.

Colophon

The animal on the cover of *Sencha Touch 2 Up and Running* is a kultarr.

The cover image is from *Meyers Kleines Lexicon*. The cover font is Adobe ITC Garamond. The text font is Adobe Minion Pro; the heading font is Adobe Myriad Condensed; and the code font is Dalton Maag's Ubuntu Mono.

Have it your way.

Get even more for your money.

Join the O'Reilly Community, and register the O'Reilly books you own. It's free, and you'll get:

- $4.99 ebook upgrade offer
- 40% upgrade offer on O'Reilly print books
- Membership discounts on books and events
- Free lifetime updates to ebooks and videos
- Multiple ebook formats, DRM FREE
- Participation in the O'Reilly community
- Newsletters
- Account management
- 100% Satisfaction Guarantee

Signing up is easy:

1. **Go to: oreilly.com/go/register**
2. **Create an O'Reilly login.**
3. **Provide your address.**
4. **Register your books.**

Note: English-language books only

To order books online:
oreilly.com/store

For questions about products or an order:
orders@oreilly.com

To sign up to get topic-specific email announcements and/or news about upcoming books, conferences, special offers, and new technologies:
elists@oreilly.com

For technical questions about book content:
booktech@oreilly.com

To submit new book proposals to our editors:
proposals@oreilly.com

O'Reilly books are available in multiple DRM-free ebook formats. For more information:
oreilly.com/ebooks

Spreading the knowledge of innovators   oreilly.com

Lightning Source UK Ltd.
Milton Keynes UK
UKOW05f1249271117
313432UK00005B/552/P